CRACKS
IN THE
FOUNDATION

**REFUTING THE CONSERVATIVE CASE FOR
LOW TAXES AND SMALL GOVERNMENT**

ELAINE J. HANDELMAN

Beaver's Pond Press, Inc.
Edina Minnesota

Cracks in the Foundation © copyright 2004 by Elaine J. Handelman. All rights reserved. No part of this book may be reproduced in any form whatsoever, by photography or xerography or by any other means, by broadcast or transmission, by translation into any kind of language, nor by recording electronically or otherwise, without permission in writing from the author, except by a reviewer, who may quote brief passages in critical articles or reviews.

ISBN 1-59298-083-X

Library of Congress Catalog Number: 2004113325

Printed in the United States of America

First Printing: October 2004

08 07 06 05 04   6 5 4 3 2 1

Cover and interior design by Rachel Holscher
Typesetting by Stanton Publication Services, Inc.

Beaver's Pond Press, Inc.

7104 Ohms Lane, Suite 216
Edina, MN 55439-2129
(952) 829-8818
www.BeaversPondPress.com

to order, visit www.BookHouseFulfillment.com or call 1-800-901-3480. Reseller discounts available.

to SHOSHANA *and* DAVID

my inspirations

Acknowledgements

Thanks for permission to quote: Council of State Governments, The Foundation Center, Giving USA 2003, published by AAFRC Trust for Philanthropy, Gartner, Inc., and General Electric Corporation.

Thanks to Kurt Burch for editing, Oksana Leukhina for help with economic data, Susan I. D. Miller, Seth Weston-Stuart for research assistance, and to many, many librarians whose work is essential to our freedom.

Contents

CHAPTER ONE ▶ The Why, What, and How of This Book ▶ 1

CHAPTER TWO ▶ One Hundred Years of Taxes—
Charting the Century ▶ 7

CHAPTER THREE ▶ What About Hong Kong?
The Tax Burden's of Other Nations ▶ 21

CHAPTER FOUR ▶ The Twentieth Century Tradeoff—
Freedom and Government ▶ 29

CHAPTER FIVE ▶ Myths of Government and Business ▶ 49

CHAPTER SIX ▶ Of Charity and Faith ▶ 69

CHAPTER SEVEN ▶ How One State Has Fared ▶ 87

CHAPTER EIGHT ▶ Comments, Concerns, and Conclusions ▶ 103

Appendix I ▶ 119

Notes ▶ 129

Index ▶ 149

CHAPTER ONE

The Why, What, and How of This Book

When I began to read *National Review* in the early 1960s, I did so surreptitiously. No one of my friends was conservative, and they perceived those on the right as wrong, stupid and racist. Among my friends reading such a journal would have cast suspicion on my liberal credentials but even more on my intelligence and tolerance. Yet I also knew that my Cousin Sheila in New York, then a devotee of Ayn Rand, was very bright and definitely not a racist. I started to read William F. Buckley's magazine because I wanted to argue with someone, and the *National Review* was then the only conservative periodical I could find.

During my subscription, I found that the *Review* had at least one other liberal reader: Murray Kempton. I was also reading the *New Republic* in those days, and enjoyed his work in that journal very much. After a few years of reading both journals, I remained in the liberal fold, but I concluded something quite different from my peers about conservatives. Certainly some conservatives were headline-grabbing, right wing bigots—those were the days of the Civil Rights Movement—but their number included intelligent, principled, and non-racist members as well. If I was not convinced by their arguments, then I did come to respect their views. And as readers of the *National Review* in those days would appreciate, I also increased my vocabulary, especially of Latin words!

Fast forward to the end of the twentieth century. If liberals still hold the views about conservatives that they did in the 1960s, then they have their heads in the sand. There are now more—it seems many more—conservative think tanks than liberal ones. The right convincingly achieved political power with the election of President Reagan, and it has been on the march since. While there is still the occasional dopey sounding bigot, there are many, many more intelligent, well prepared, principled, and highly confident conservatives. Many of them now hold political office.

I have been disappointed with the liberal response to this changed political reality. I rarely read of or hear of liberals, Democrats, or other folks to the left of center dispute the assumptions of the right. I don't know if that is because they don't take conservative ideas seriously, or if in the brief time they can expect to hold the public's attention they prefer to articulate their own ideas. And most of the polemical books written—on both sides—seem to be addressed to those who share the beliefs of their authors.

The purpose of this book is to refute assumptions that almost all conservatives believe about taxes, the size of government, and the effects of both on our freedoms. I address my rebuttal to those on the right as well as those in my camp. I bring the values to this work that I have brought to my work in research and service quality in the private sector: to treat and present data fairly. Although I quote experts in some instances, I use their views sparingly and not to support arguments. The reason is as simple as it is sad. For every liberal expert, there is a conservative one, and it seems nothing is gained by quoting one side. For the same reason, I avoid theories and models.

In laying out my case, I use economic and other data that is widely available and widely accepted, e.g. Statistical Abstract of the United States and World Bank statistics. I concentrate on the twentieth century where relevant information is reasonably complete and add occasional updates to the present. This work is not comprehensive. I believe I provide enough information to cast serious doubt on conservative views, but I have not exhausted the subject. My hunch is that most readers will prefer the amount of detail I provide over an exhaustive treatment.

To deal with the issues of taxes and government size and efficiency, it is necessary to present and discuss numbers. Being aware that some readers are number-phobic, I use graphs to represent quantitative information where possible. Numbers are prominent in only a few chapters.

To be clear about the purpose of this work, the following is a brief summary of the issues I challenge.

Conservatives believe that government costs too much and does too much. Whether libertarian or religious conservative, there is consensus on the right that if taxes were lower and government were smaller, we would all be much better off.

In the view of the Right, money paid to the government diverts funds which would be better spent investing in new and existing enterprises. When we have to part with a portion of our earnings, we feel less reward for our efforts. That feeling in turn, reduces our incentive to invest more and to work harder. Free enterprise, unfettered by high taxes and excessive regulation, increases the nation's wealth, and reduces the need for government largesse. Local or private means best address those problems that increased wealth itself cannot tackle.

Conservatives regard big government as inefficient, ineffective, and unresponsive. Big government does not provide solutions; it creates burdens. As Ronald Reagan, the most revered of conservatives, put it, "The Washington Establishment is not the answer. It's the problem." In his first inaugural speech he went on to say, "It is no coincidence that our present troubles parallel and are proportionate to the intervention and intrusion in our lives that result from unnecessary and excessive growth of government." In these speeches Reagan was addressing the twin problems of inflation and unemployment, but the right now regards these statements as general truths. In fact, Reagan asserted, "The truth is that outside of its legitimate function, government does nothing as well or as economically as the private sector." In other words, when we transfer work from government to the private sector we will find that it is done better and more cheaply. For example, conservatives believe that helping the needy with private largesse or with faith-based initiatives will be more effective than what has been provided by public aid.

Implicit in the critique of government is a belief in the effectiveness and efficiency of the free enterprise system and of for-profit organizations. Most Americans share this view, and with good reason. The capitalist system has greatly expanded the wealth of our nation and many others. Yet when the market functions less well than expected or produces undesired results, then conservatives say excessive regulation and/or taxation is the cause. The market itself is never at fault. Conservatives' "faith" in the free market system and in private enterprises at times borders on the religious. The depth of their belief is reminiscent of that held by ideologists of the Left.

To dismiss the conservative attitude towards government and taxes as arising from simple greed is to misunderstand and underestimate it. The right is principled and well-prepared. Conservatives believe that more government means less freedom. Dollars paid as taxes are dollars that can't be spent or saved according to the discretion of the citizen. Governments that collect unnecessary taxes are coercive. Indeed government itself is generally coercive, almost an evil empire. Citizens should tolerate a loss of freedom only when the nation is at peril. Grover Norquist, one of the nation's most powerful conservative activists, calls the organizations he coordinates the "leave us alone" coalition.

Many will be thinking that to be left alone, to have fewer hassles from government, and to pay less in taxes are conditions to be welcomed. We all would prefer fewer rules and regulations, and we certainly would prefer to pay fewer taxes. But would we be better off?

My answer is that we would not, and the purpose of this book is to show you why. Adopting the conservative paradigm will have deleterious effects on our economy, on our personal lives and on our social fabric. In the coming pages I offer evidence to show that the conservative vision for this nation is based upon faulty assumptions. I argue that we have come to require—not just desire—far more services from government than ever before for both our economic and personal well-being. The right's assumption that continuously lowering taxes will make us wealthier is based on faith, not fact.

We may occasionally improve on what government provides by relying on the private sector, but that will by no means be the automatically preferable solution. The private sector is not the paragon of competence and efficiency that conservative ideologues allege. The popularity of the cartoon character Dilbert is one indication of that. But corporations can improve themselves, and so can government. The solution to both bad business and bad government is not to destroy either, but to improve both. I will also demonstrate that it is unrealistic to expect that private largesse can adequately care for the needy in our society.

I ask those who have concluded that government is an "evil empire" to consider whether they would prefer to get along without some of the government's contributions over the last century. Finally, having lived in a state led by a governor who has signed a no tax increase pledge, I describe some of the local effects of this brave new conservative world. In my concluding chapter, I summarize my position and offer observations on several subjects including the president's expressed and unexpressed views about taxes, new attitudes toward the poor, and good and bad government reform.

CHAPTER TWO

One Hundred Years of Taxes —
Charting the Century

The usual way to express how heavily a nation is taxed is to calculate tax burden. For many years the Tax Foundation has calculated this burden. This conservative, educational organization created Tax Freedom Day, the day of the year when Americans earn "enough money to pay off their total tax bill for the year." In 1940 that date was March 5, in 1960 it was April 9, and in 2000 it was May 2.[1] The Tax Foundation's method of calculating tax burden (total taxes collected as a percent of total income) is one of several.* For purposes of this chapter it is perfectly adequate.

I use charts to present tax burden and other economic data. By doing so, we can look at changes over a long period of time — in our case, a century — without having to deal with a lot of numbers. Figure 2.1 shows the Tax Foundation's calculation of tax burden over the twentieth century.

---

*All such calculations are averages and approximations. They are averages because they lump all taxes together into one total, take some measure of our combined incomes, and then divide the first total by the second one. They are approximations because they do not tell us anything about the distribution of taxes, i.e. how much falls on business compared to individuals and how progressive the tax rates are, etc.

Figure 2.1
Tax Burden for the United States over the Twentieth Century[2]

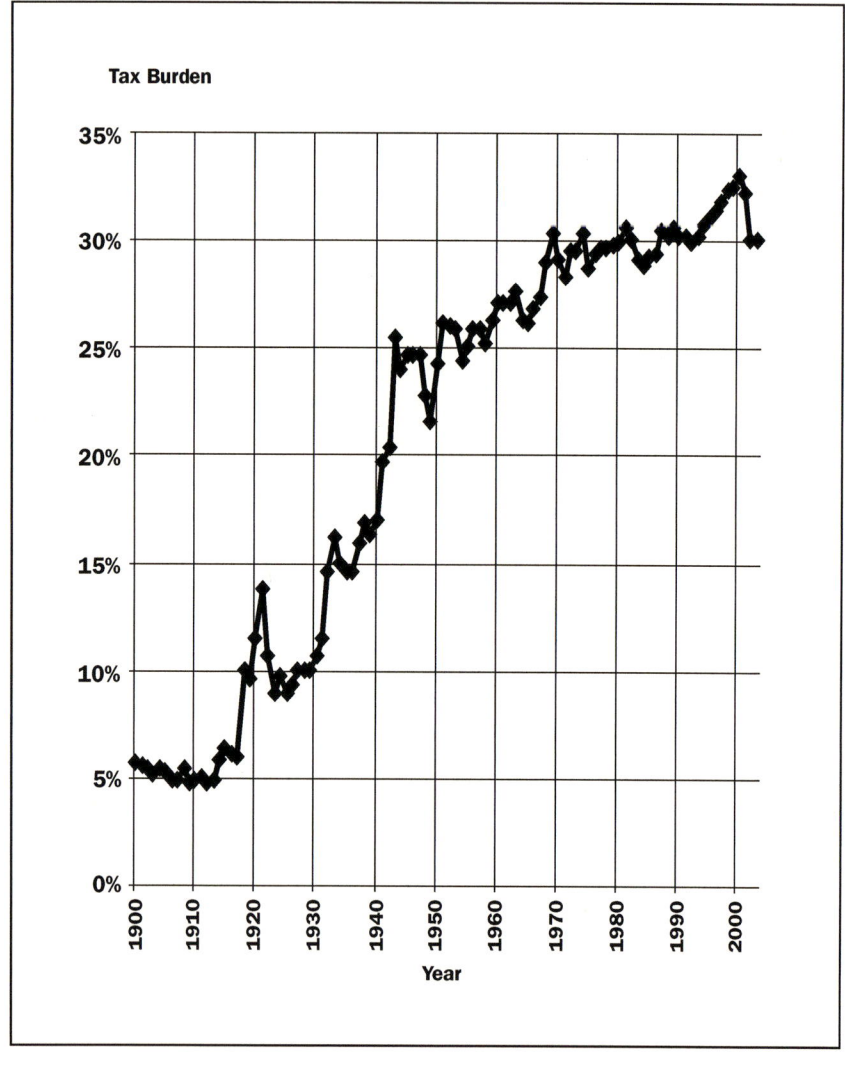

After a flat or declining period for the first fifteen years, the tax burden rose for much of the century, albeit at differing rates. The increases and decreases before and after World Wars One and Two are prominent. In contrast to our war in Iraq, both of those wars were financed with taxes and debt.

The greatest peace-time increase in the tax burden occurred during the Depression. Compared to that era, the increase in tax burden during 1970s and 1980s was quite small. Tax revenues began to climb more steeply in the nineties, and we experienced our highest tax burden of the century in 1999 and 2000, when, according to the Tax Foundation's calculations, it reached 34 percent.

For those who remember congressional debates over tax policy it is striking to see how small the effect of tax legislation seems in this century view. The Kennedy/Johnson tax cut of 1964 led to a slightly lower tax burden for a few years. The effect of the large 1981 Reagan tax cut is evident even though mitigated by a large tax increase a year later. The tax increase of 1993 and the expansion of the nineties combined to increase the tax burden throughout the rest of the decade.

Figure 2.2 compares the Federal portion of the tax burden to the total tax burden.

It's clear that the Federal portion of our tax burden grew quite slowly from the 1950s until the early 1990s. The run-up apparent after that corresponds with the economic boom we enjoyed. That was an expansion that conservatives predicted would not occur. Why? Because a tax increase was enacted in 1993, the minimum wage was raised twice during the period, and the tax burden continued to rise to the end of the century. The expansion that did occur was a lollapalooza. Unemployment dipped to levels unknown for decades. Venture capital flowed like water. The stock market had itself quite a bubble. The Federal deficit was eliminated, and, for the first time since 1960 we enjoyed a U.S. federal budget surplus. One can only wonder what might have happened had

Figure 2.2
Total Tax Burden and Federal Tax Burden for the United States over the Twentieth Century[3]

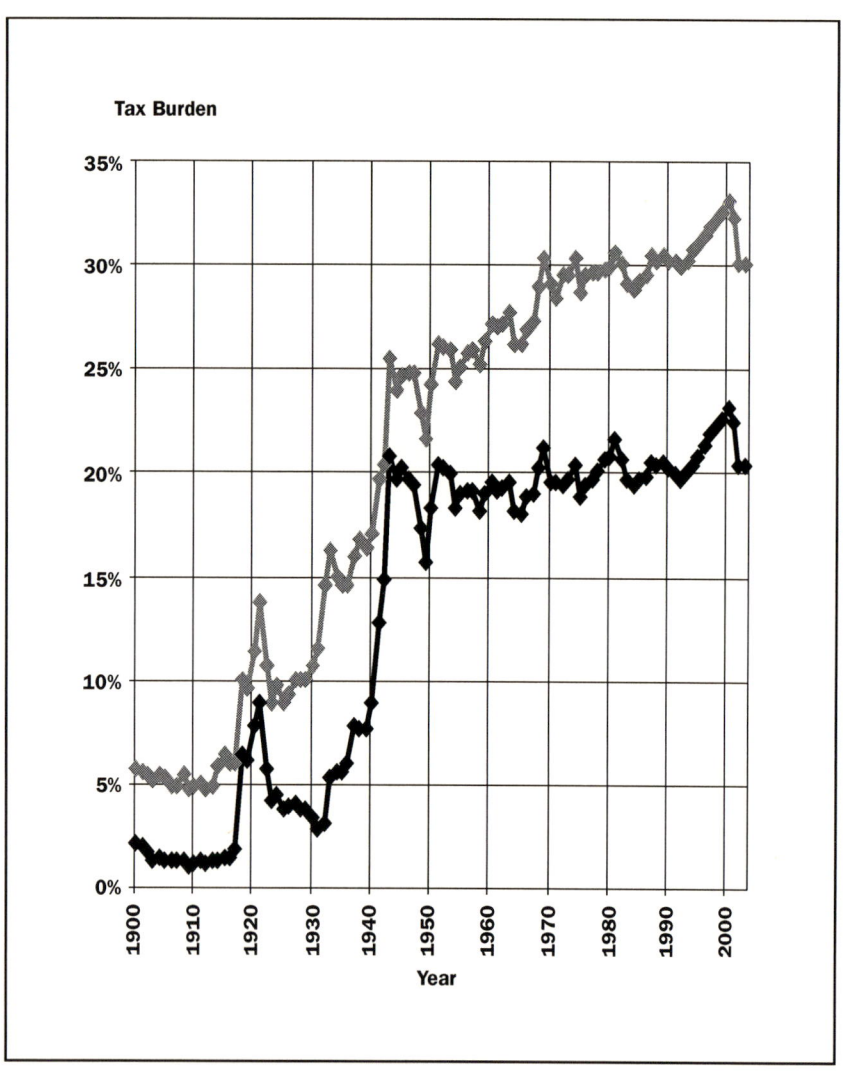

there not been a shortage of individuals with technical skills, particularly in the newer areas of information technology.

Figure 2.3 compares the burden of state and local taxes to the total tax burden.

Two periods of increasing tax burden are apparent in Figure 2.3. State and local taxes accounted for a substantial portion of the growth in tax burden during the Depression. Also, the increasing state and local tax burden that occurred during the period between World War II and 1970 was a justification for the State and Local Fiscal Assistance Act of 1972, commonly called the Revenue Sharing Act. The financial needs of many of our large cities had become too great to be met using their traditional sources of revenue: property and sales taxes. During the rest of that decade, however, revenue sharing declined in importance as inflation diluted its impact.

Having briefly looked at tax burden over the last century, we can now turn to economic growth over the same period. The most popular measure of economic growth is gross domestic product (GDP). GDP is the market value of all final goods and services produced in the country in one year. GDP must be adjusted to reflect real change, not change in the value of money. Figure 2.4 shows the growth of real GDP[5] over the twentieth century.

Clearly, with the exception of the Depression years, the US economy has been growing very well during most of the century. Caplow, Hicks and Wattenberg, authors of *The First Measured Century*,[7] called U.S. economic growth in the twentieth century "phenomenal."

Another measure of the economy's growth, a non-financial one, is the growth in new patents seen in Figure 2.5. This reflects the development of new products and processes, a major factor in the creation of wealth.

While the growth in the number of patents issued has been irregular during the century, the dramatic rise in patents during the last two

Figure 2.3
Total Tax Burden and Average State and Local Tax Burden for the United States over the Twentieth Century[4]

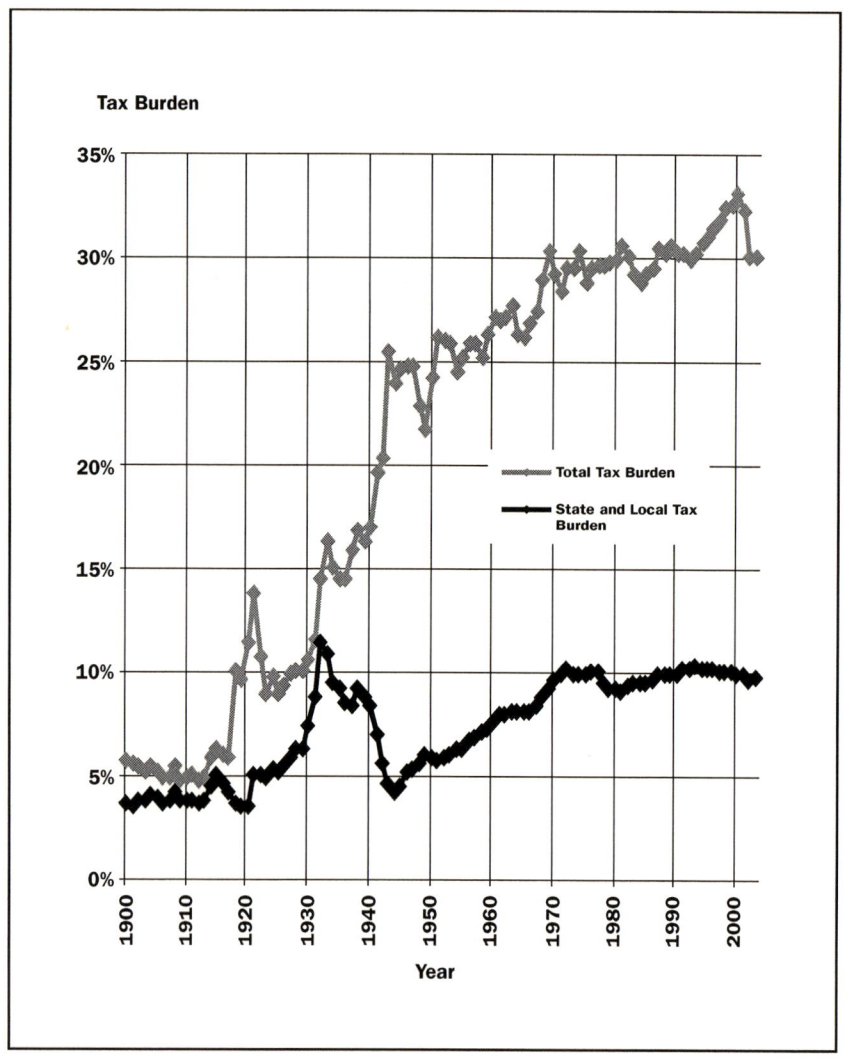

Figure 2.4
Tax Burden and Growth of the Real GDP (in 2000 dollars) during the Twentieth Century[6]

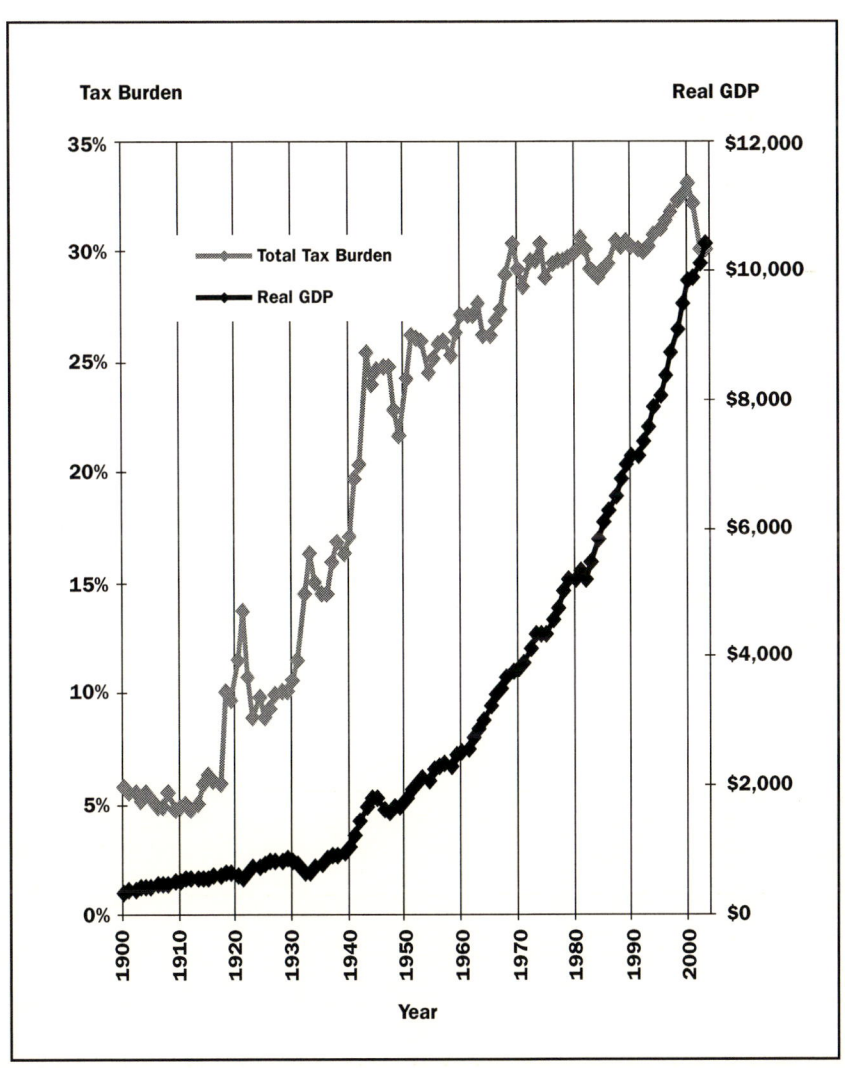

Figure 2.5
Tax Burden and New Patents per Year Issued to US Individuals and Corporations during the Twentieth Century[8]

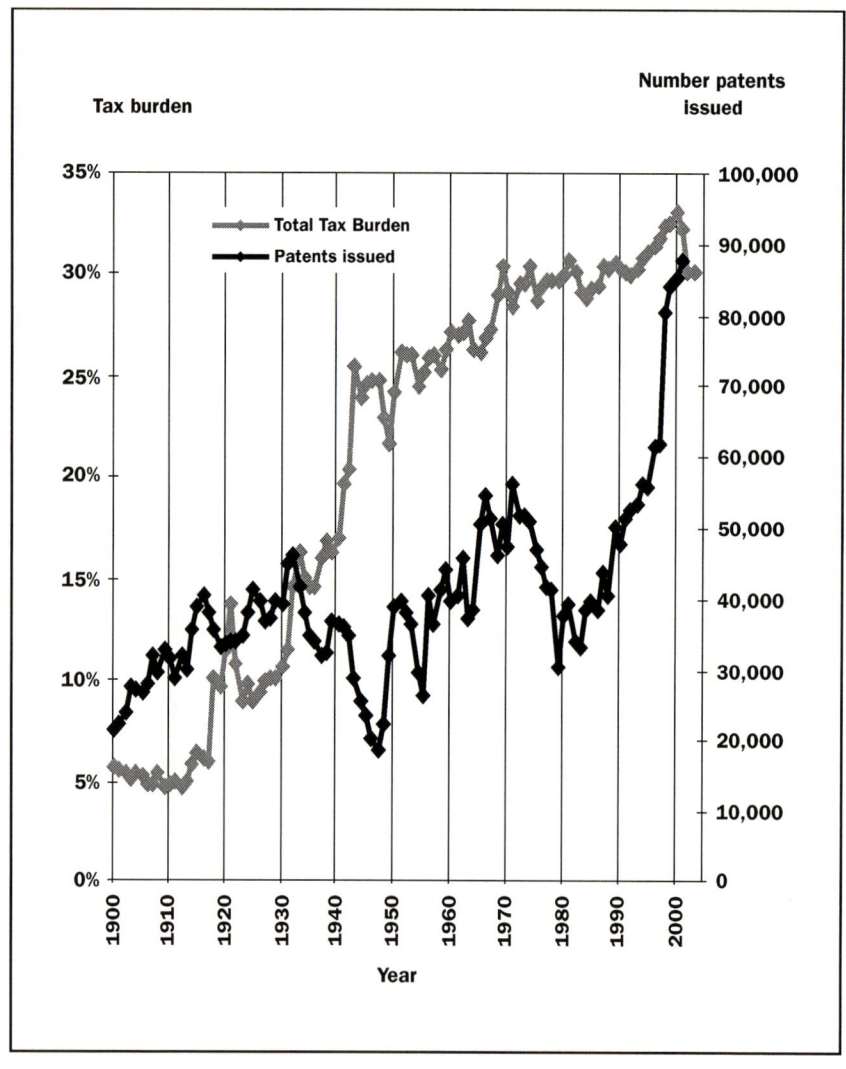

decades when the tax burden was its highest suggests the tax burden during those years did not impede research, innovation, and subsequent patenting.

Economic growth waxes and wanes in what is called the business cycle. Figure 2.6 shows the business cycles during the twentieth century. The two longest peace-time expansions during the twentieth century occurred at the end of the century when the tax burden was nearing its peak.

Finally, and most importantly, look at the effect of tax burden on our standard of living. An economy can grow simply because of population growth, since growing numbers of people must pay rent, buy food and purchase detergent to wash clothes, etc. In that case the standard of living does not rise. When the economy grows faster than the population, then we experience an improved standard of living. Figure 2.7 shows the increase in the most widely accepted measure of standard of living, real GDP per capita.

This figure demonstrates quite clearly that as our tax burden was rising over the century, so was our standard of living. Those who insist that taxes suppress the incentive to work and the ability to invest would predict eventual economic malaise with such an increasing tax burden. Instead, we have one of the highest standards of living in the world today, and the two longest peace-time economic expansions of the century occurred when tax burden was at its highest. The American economy has produced more wealth for its citizens than any country at any time in human history! And yet, even after economic growth of the 1990s proved the conservatives wrong, the right continues to complain about the damaging effect of taxes on our economy.

The continuing conservative complaint about taxes even in the absence of good evidence is understandable. If our tax burden hasn't prevented our unparalleled prosperity, then tax increases at some future time could be considered. That's not a welcome prospect for any of us. But for conservatives, it would be a calamity. A tax increase raises

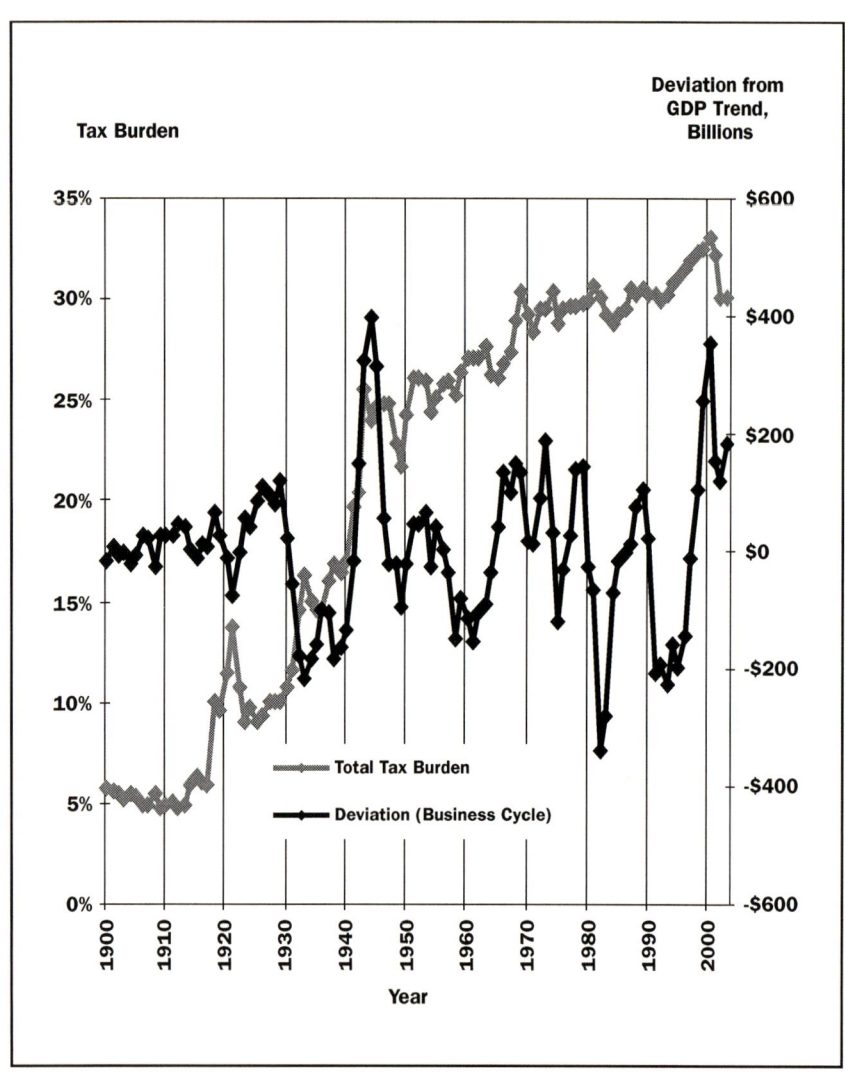

Figure 2.6
The Tax Burden and Business Cycles during the Twentieth Century[9]

Figure 2.7
Tax Burden and Average Annual GDP per capita (in 2000 dollars) during the Twentieth Century[10]

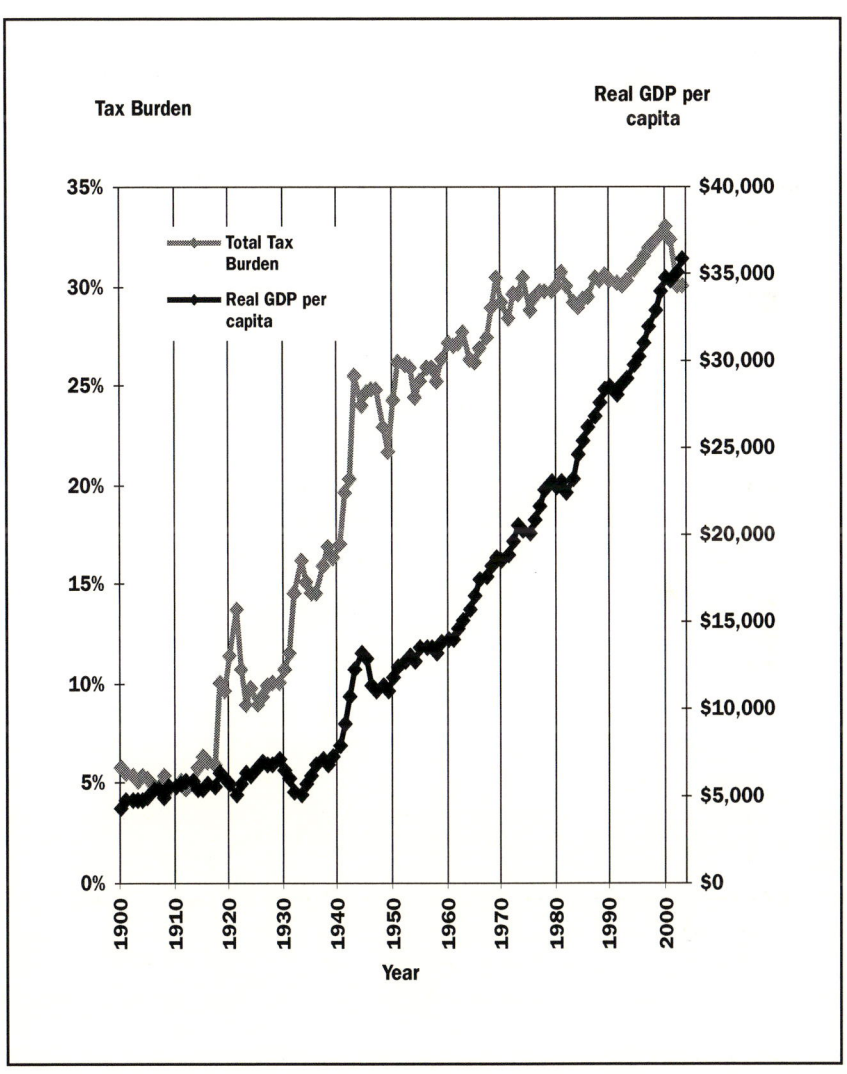

the possibility that government could do more and become larger. The Right is against increasing government size.

Many who don't share conservatives' convictions about taxation nevertheless hope that we can manage our nation's needs with fewer taxes and with less government. There is widespread belief that government can't be trusted, and that it wastes a lot of our hard-earned money. So if we put the screws to it, maybe we can get what we need while giving up less of our incomes. It's a view that has been seducing citizens for many years.

Actually, conservatives who have looked carefully at modern economies know perfectly well that the tax burden is but one of many factors that contribute to a nation's economic health. For example, the conservative Heritage Foundation and *The Wall Street Journal* have been producing an Index of Economic Freedom[11] for ten years. "The best path to economic development and rising living standards," *The Wall Street Journal* wrote in 2004, "is the one paved with economic freedom."[12] The Index measures a total of ten factors, including tax burden. Most significantly, all factors are given *equal* weight. Besides tax burden they are: trade policy, government intervention in the economy, monetary policy, capital flows and foreign investment, banking and finance, wages and prices, property rights, regulation, and black market activity.[13]

The Heritage Foundation's Index of Economic Freedom for 2004 ranks the city-states of Hong Kong and Singapore as numbers one and two, respectively, in the list of over 150 countries rated. Hong Kong has held the top position since the Index began. More surprising, Sweden and Denmark are in the top fifteen this year, and they have received high ratings for many other years as well. Yet these countries have tax burdens that are among the highest in the world. The Organization for Economic Co-operation and Development (OECD) defines tax burden as taxes collected as a percent of GDP.* According to their calculations, Sweden's and Denmark's tax burdens in the year 2000 were 54.0%

and 49.5% respectively compared to 29.7% for the United States in the same year.[14]

Though some nations have managed very well with high tax burdens, everyone agrees that taxes can not be increased endlessly. Excessive tax rates can stifle economic growth by reducing incentives and availability of capital. And if taxes are too low and government doesn't provide needed services, then economic growth can also be adversely affected. There is also consensus that the manner in which the tax burden is distributed on businesses and individuals has economic consequences. But most on the Right do not clamor for tax redistribution; their call is simply to lower taxes.

Conservatives' conviction that we would have been better off had taxes been lower is part of their belief system. Yet we know that relatively high taxes and economic prosperity went hand in hand in the 1990s. Over the hundred years of the twentieth century, the U.S. tax burden increased between five and six fold while our standard of living (measured as GDP per capita) in real dollars (adjusted for inflation) increased even more, seven fold. What will conservatives say about that?

Though tax burden hasn't been the millstone around the neck of our economy that conservatives allege, other questions remain. Have other economies been more prosperous or grown faster than our own? If so, have they managed with lower tax burdens? I take up that topic in the next chapter.

---

*OECD cautions that comparisons between countries are approximate because of the varying ways that taxes, particularly social welfare taxes, are reported.

CHAPTER THREE

What About Hong Kong?
The Tax Burdens of Other Nations

Conservatives used to extol Hong Kong for its wonderful economy and low tax rates. The success of this city-state, formerly a colony of Great Britain and now a part of China, has been impressive, but it is no longer the economic star it once was. Its shining skyscrapers fail to reflect new realities. Hong Kong's average annual economic growth between 1995 and 2000 was just under 1 percent per year compared with our 3.2 percent per year during the same period.[1] Hong Kong's 1994 unemployment was 1.9 percent; in early 2004 it was 7.9 percent. The nation's economic problems may be related to the financial crises that staggered Asia in 1997-1998, but blame may also be found within. For example, "powerful family-owned conglomerates enjoy virtual monopolies in everything from shipping to real-estate development to supermarkets in the territory." The resulting "lack of competition contributes to higher fuel, food and real-estate prices."[2] Apparently for conservatives these monopolies and high prices were minor considerations compared to Hong Kong's tax burden.

This chapter compares today's economic standouts to those most in need of improvement to see what kind of tax burdens they have. Then we look at what kind of relationship exists between standard of living and economic growth. I rely on the well-known sources for international economic data, the Organization for Economic Cooperation and Development (OECD)[3], and the International Monetary Fund (IMF)[4]. The OECD and IMF define tax burden as total tax revenue as a percentage of GDP.*[5]

The nation with the highest standard of living at the end of the twentieth century was little Luxembourg. Its GDP per capita in 2000 was $53,410.** This nation's recent successes in banking have more than replaced the decline of its steel industry.[6] In 2000 its tax burden was

Table 3.1
The Ten Countries with the Highest Standards of Living (GDP per capita) in the Year 2000 and their Tax Burdens[5]

Country	Standard of Living (in PPP adjusted U.S. dollars)*	Tax burden, percent
Luxembourg	$53,410	40.4
United States	$33,293	29.7
Ireland	$30,380	31.2
Norway	$29,200	39.0
Iceland	$28,910	38.3
Denmark	$28,680	49.5
Switzerland	$27,780	31.2
Netherlands	$26,910	41.1
Canada	$26,840	35.6
Austria	$26,420	43.3

*For details of data selected, see footnote 5.

**Expressed in U.S. dollars adjusted by purchasing power parity (PPP) calculations rather than by conversion at official currency exchange rates. The PPP method is widely used in international economic comparisons, because it depends on the power of a nation's currency to purchase local goods and services.

40.4 percent, compared to the 29.7 percent for the United States. As with most prosperous European countries, it has a national health care system. The other standouts, the "standard-of-living top ten for the year 2000," are shown in Table 3.1.

The main conclusion from Table 3.1 is that most countries with high standards of living have tax burdens greater than our own. Six of the ten, Luxembourg, Ireland, Denmark, Switzerland, the United States and Canada are in the Heritage Foundation's list of free economies.[7] In this top ten list (from a total of 208 countries) all but the United States have nationalized health care systems. That accounts, in part, for the higher tax burdens in this group. According to OECD statistics, the United States spent 13.1 percent of its GDP on health care in 2000.[8] If U.S. tax burden

Table 3.2

Ten Countries with Moderate Standards of Living (GDP per capita) in the Year 2000 and their Tax Burdens[5]

Country	Standard of Living (in PPP adjusted U.S. dollars)*	Tax burden, percent
Panama	$5,830	18.0
Kazakhstan	$5,720	19.3
Iran	$5,720	16.2
Venezuela, RB	$5,580	12.8
Romania	$5,500	29.7
Belize	$5,470	16.3
St. Vincent and the Grenadines	$5,350	26.4
El Salvador	$5,240	10.9
Guatemala	$4,430	10.2
Swaziland	$4,330	27.6

is combined with its health care "burden" the result is approximately 42.7 percent or well within the range of the tax burdens found in Table 3.1.

Table 3.2 shows ten countries with standard of living in the midrange of the 208 countries in IMF's World Development Indicators database. Those with high tax burdens (Romania, St. Vincent and the Grenadines and Swaziland) devote a substantial amount of government funds to health care, but so do others such as Panama. In general, tax burdens are lower for these nations than they are for those with the highest standards of living. These ten "moderate" countries have tax burdens similar to Hong Kong's 17.5%,[9] but these nations support defense forces, and Hong Kong does not.

Comparing nations with high, medium, and low standards of living

Table 3.3
Ten Countries with Low Standards of Living (GDP per capita) in the Year 2000 and their Tax Burdens[5]

Country	Standard of Living (in PPP adjusted U.S. dollars)*	Tax burden, percent
Pakistan	$1,870	17.7
Ivory Coast	$1,550	10.5
Senegal	$1,450	8.7
Uganda	$1,450	6.0
Nepal	$1,280	11.1
Congo, Rep.	$950	6.2
Madagascar	$810	13.1
Yemen	$800	10.5
Burundi	$680	15.8
Sierra Leone	$450	12.1

(see Tables 3.1, 3.2, and 3.3) makes clear that tax burden varies with standard of living. While the data presented doesn't prove a causal relationship, it should caution those who believe lower tax burdens are always better. Results of this admittedly small study suggest they are not.

Table 3.4 shows the tax burdens for countries whose economies grew the most between 1995 and 2000.

Table 3.4
Tax Burden in the Year 2000 and Average Annual Growth for the Period 1995–2000 for Nations with the Highest Average Growth[10]

Country	Average annual growth of real GDP per capita, percent	Tax burden, percent
Belarus	9	27
Ireland	9	31
Tajikistan	8	10
Dominican Republic	7	13
China	6	15
Kazakhstan	5	19
Latvia	5	31
Luxembourg	5	40
Estonia	5	33
Poland	5	34

Of these ten countries with the highest growth rates in 1995–2000, four had tax burdens significantly lower than the United States. The rest had tax burdens nearly as high as or higher than ours. This sample suggests that a low tax burden is not a requirement for robust economic growth. Notice that two of the countries in this list, Luxembourg and Ireland, were also in the standard-of-living top ten.

The economic stardom that Hong Kong used to enjoy deserves now to shine on Ireland. For generations this nation was known for its poetry, prose, and steady stream of people emigrating for better economic opportunities. But in the last decade of the twentieth century, Ireland became the "Celtic Tiger" because of its rapid economic development, mainly in the information technology sector. Whether in Dublin or Galway, upscale shops and construction cranes proliferated. Well-educated, computer-literate Irish young people became the well-dressed owners of new condominiums. For the first time, emigrants began to return. By 1999, Ireland's GDP per capita exceeded that of England. Its tax burden in 2000 was a bit higher than that of the United States. With that tax burden the Irish, however, receive far more health care benefits from their government than do U.S. citizens.

Finally, Figure 3.1 shows the relationship—actually the lack of a relationship—between standard of living and economic growth for 138 countries.

The horizontal axis shows the average standard of living (average GDP per capita) during the period of 1995 through 2000 of 138 nations. One can see that the U.S. has the second highest value. The vertical axis shows the average growth of the standard of living (average GDP per capita) during the period of 1995 through 2000 for the same countries. Most of the points in Figure 3.1 are clustered between growth rates of zero and 4% for average GDP per capita per year (along the vertical axis) and between zero and about $10,000 average GDP per capita (along the horizontal axis). What one does not see is any tendency for Average Growth of GDP per capita to increase or decrease as standard of living (Average GDP per capita) increases. As one moves to the right, there is no tendency for data points be either higher or lower along the vertical axis. That means that the two quantities graphed are

Figure 3.1
Scatter Plot of Average Annual Growth of Standard of Living (1995–2000) and Average Standard of Living (1995–2000) for 138 Countries[11]

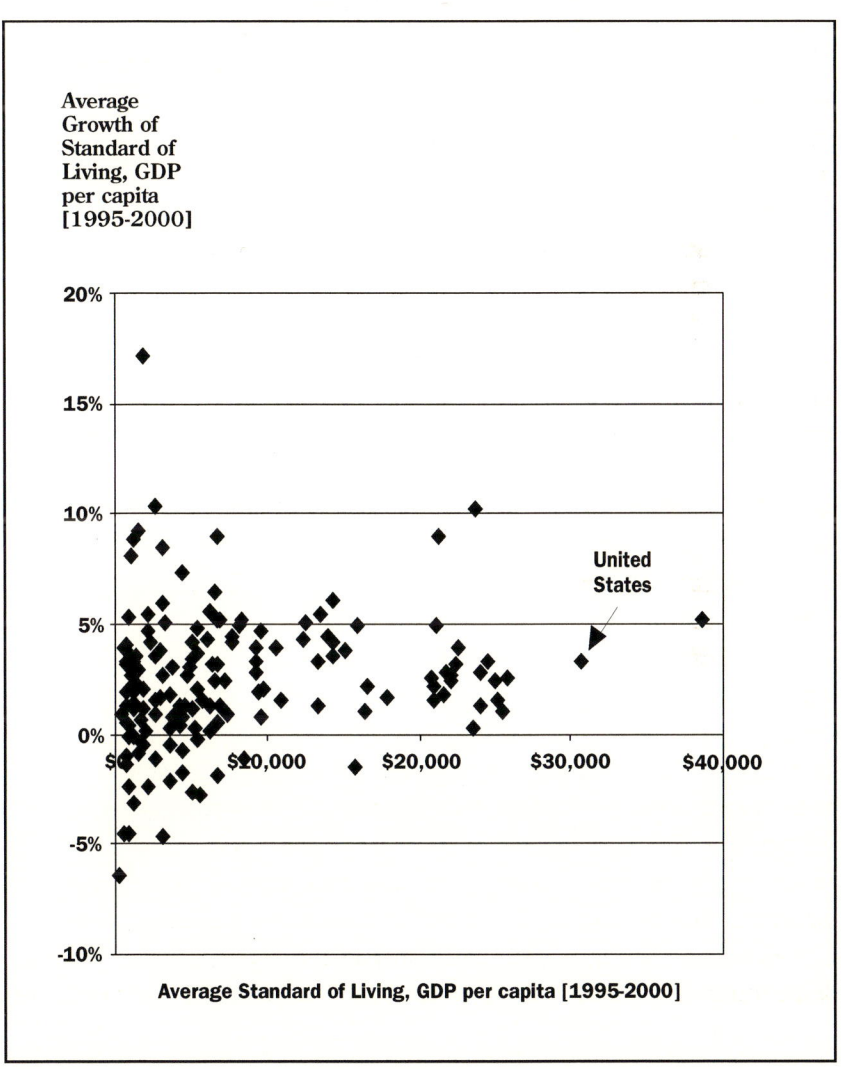

not related. They are independent of one another. This lack of relationship is well known and widely accepted among economists.

From data presented in this chapter, we can conclude that in recent years:

- most prosperous nations have higher tax burdens than our own.
- most poor countries have tax burdens lower than we have.
- some nations which are growing faster than the United States have lower tax burdens than ours, but more do not.
- there is no relationship between growth of standard of living and standard of living.

While the facts provided do not disprove the notion that lowering our tax burden will lead to higher economic growth and a higher standard of living, they do cast serious doubt on these widely held conservative assumptions. When those on the right predict better economic results with lower taxes, we need to ask for evidence. It is likely to be found in the economic models of conservative economists, not in the real world.

I next take up the issues of what government does and how freedom is affected.

CHAPTER FOUR

The Twentieth Century Tradeoff—
Freedom and Government

Consider two average Americans adults living in the year 1900. Let's call them Jack and Molly. Jack probably worked on a farm or at some sort of manual labor. Molly was much less likely to work outside the home than Jack, but if she did, she too probably worked either on a farm or in some other occupation which required working with her hands (such as maid or cook). If Jack worked in the manufacturing industry, then his work week is likely to have been fifty-nine hours, the average at the time for that kind of labor. If he was one of the few who belonged to a union or worked for the Post Office, then he would have worked fewer hours and earned more per hour[1].

The odds were less than one in ten that either of these adults had a high school diploma. At that time very few jobs required that much education; only eighteen percent of the labor force had white collar jobs.[2] If Jack happened to be well educated he could expect to be hired by a corporation provided he was white and Protestant. He would have applied using the name John. For Jack and Molly the two day weekend was unknown.

Though there was much less free time at the beginning of the century than we have now, Jack and Molly still had many options for leisure:

picnics, swimming, baseball, the occasional theater or circus, and reading. The printed word was also the way—the only way—to learn of current events. Jack might have dreamt of retiring to a life of leisure, but with life expectancy less than fifty years (and for African-Americans much less than forty years), the odds of his fulfilling that dream were not good. Jack had an income of $4,700 (in 2000 dollars), and paid very few taxes. The income tax would not be legal until 1913. He could vote, but Molly could not, and in many places he would be unlikely to have had that right if he were an African American.

By the end of the century, voting had been extended to all American citizens. Discrimination on the basis of race, creed, ethnicity, or gender is against the law. The forty-hour work week is taken for granted, because The Fair Labor Standards Act enacted in 1938 required overtime pay for time worked weekly beyond forty hours. The printed word is but one of many ways we use to learn about the world. Newspapers are considered the best way to follow current events, but also the most expensive of the media. Life expectancy is just over seventy-five years, which gives most of us an opportunity to retire and choose how to spend our retirement years. Average per capita income in the United States was close to $35,000 in 2000, and the average tax burden was 34 percent (in the Tax Foundation's estimation). If freedom varies with the portion of our income we keep, then we were freer in 1900. Yet most of us, I suspect, would prefer the freedom we had in 2000. The income we kept at the end of the century provided us with many more choices than the average person had in 1900: what to read, what to wear, what to eat, what to learn, where to learn, where to live, where to work, how to entertain ourselves, etc. The capacity to exercise choice is an important part of our freedom, and there is no question that the number and quality of choices increased over the century.

To be sure, the freedom of choice we enjoy results in part from the growth of the U.S. economy. But that growth would not have been possible without significant investments in the public sector. Our increased longevity, for example, owes much to medical advances and public health measures. In at least two areas, transportation and education, funds diverted from our pockets to the government led directly and indirectly to increased choices for many of us.

Federal expenditures on construction of roads, highways, and bridges have become commonplace. Earlier in our history such projects were carried out by individual states or private companies. The most famous of these was New York's Erie Canal. The state of New York completed the project after a private venture failed. One of many canals built, the Erie was completed in 1825. Canals were the highways of the early nineteenth century. The Erie Canal "turned New York Harbor into America's number one port, and it shaped the social and economic development of the nation. Shipping costs dropped dramatically, immigrants to America, in search of new lands and new opportunities in the west, crowded canal boats. Cities and industries along the canal developed and flourished."[3]

The beneficial economic effects of early transportation projects such as the Erie Canal are mirrored in public transportation projects in our era. The most ambitious was the Interstate Highway Act of 1956, passed during the administration of President Eisenhower. The federal government pays for eighty or ninety percent (occasionally one hundred percent) of the costs. It is funded by a federal tax on gasoline and other excise taxes. The interstate highway system provides enormous economic opportunities and choices to U.S. citizens. It makes every private automobile more valuable, useful and desirable. The improved safety of the interstate system over other roads led to a further explosion of car-buying by Americans. Highways and cars led to suburbs, home-building, and increased demand for consumer goods like furniture, washing machines, dryers, refrigerators, stoves and televisions to fill these homes. Highways and cars also led to land developing businesses and communities, reduced delivery time for goods (which in turn reduced warehouse costs), and greater retail competition, which resulted in larger selection and lower prices, and the ability of manufacturers to serve larger markets.[4] As a result, we enjoy more choices: whether to live in a suburb or a city, where to work, where to shop, and where to vacation if we drive. Implicit in these choices was additional economic growth, which in turn produced more choices.

Creating highways is one thing; keeping them up-to-date is another. Recently elected representatives have been reluctant to maintain existing highways or provide alternative methods of transportation. Anyone living in a metropolitan area today knows the result: increasing traffic congestion. The freedom of choice we purchased with the interstate highway system and other transportation projects seems to shrink when we are repeatedly stuck in traffic. And congestion is costly. The Texas Transportation Institute (TTI) has been providing estimates of congestion costs for many years. According to TTI,[5] in 2001 "5.7 billion gallons of wasted fuel and 3.5 billion hours of lost productivity resulting from traffic congestion cost the nation $69.5 billion." TTI did not estimate the additional air pollution that congestion causes.

The failure to maintain the transportation system that so expanded Americans' freedom is documented in greater detail by the American Society of Civil Engineer's "Report Card for America's Infrastructure."[6] Their grade of D+ for U.S. roads is worse than the grade of C they give to the nation's bridges. But a grade doesn't tell the story as well as their description: As of 2000, just over one fourth of U.S. bridges were "structurally deficient or functionally obsolete . . . A structurally deficient bridge is closed or restricted to light vehicles because of its deteriorated structural components, which require speed and weight restrictions."[7]

Before the federal investment in transportation just described, the U.S. government invested in post-secondary and then secondary education. It's startling to learn that only 6.3 percent of 17 year olds were high school graduates at the beginning of the twentieth century.[8] Getting a high school diploma from a public school was a choice open to few citizens. By 1940, 49 percent of 17 year olds[9] had attended high school for four years. Currently, nearly 85 percent of adults have attended four years of high school. The percent who have attended four or more years of post-secondary education is 27.2.[10]

The commitment to secondary education, a state or local responsibility, grew gradually beginning late in the nineteenth century. Federal assistance to post-secondary education followed a very different pattern. After donating public land to states and territories in 1862 to "provide colleges for the benefit of agriculture and the mechanic arts,"[11] the federal government continued to provide some assistance to these "land grant" institutions of higher learning.

A much larger federal involvement in higher education occurred after World War Two. As part of the "G.I. Bill of Rights," veterans of the war received tuition and additional expenses to attend the college of their choice. In 1947 nearly one-half of all college students in the United States were veterans. An additional benefit of the program was to minimize the sudden entrance of a large population of unemployed young men into the job market.[12]

The next federal action to assist post-secondary education was prompted by competition from abroad, the launch in 1957 of Sputnik, the first space satellite to achieve orbit. That event made clear that the Soviet Union was ahead of the United States in important areas of science and engineering. There was a new race, the space race, and the Russians were winning. Congress passed the National Defense Education Act of 1958, which provided low interest loans for needy students, graduate fellowships, and funds for purchase of scientific equipment.

Further help for higher education began during the Kennedy-Johnson years. President Johnson had been committed to helping the underprivileged from his earliest days in public life. Grants and federally insured loan programs for low-income students begun during those years continue to the present. Over one-half of low-income students attending a college or university today receive some sort of federal assistance.

With the possible exception of the assistance to land grant universities, none of the taxpayer sponsored support for secondary and postsecondary education seems to have been motivated, at least initially, by a desire to help the American economy. But better-educated workers are essential to economic growth and productivity. As the authors of *The First Measured Century* put it, the increase in well educated Americans "represented a massive upgrading of the nation's human resources—one that enabled and sustained technological progress, the expansion of knowledge in every field, the continuing shift from blue-collar to white-collar occupations, and the adjustment to an increasingly complex social environment."[13] As with transportation, public investment in education increased our freedom in two ways. Better education not only gave individuals more choices over their lives, but also helped the economy grow. Economic growth further increased available choices. And better educated workers were more productive.

The increased productivity of American workers has been a significant factor in producing our prosperity. That productivity increase, the increase in the amount of economic goods produced by a worker in a specific amount of time, came about in part because of business investment in technological innovation and in part because of public investment in education.

An additional area worth considering here is government research and government-sponsored research. Many government organizations, such as the Department of Agriculture, Department of Commerce, and NASA support research, but the National Science Foundation (NSF) and the Defense Advanced Research Projects Agency (DARPA) are chartered specifically to conduct and support research. NSF, formed in 1950, seeks to "promote the progress of science; to advance the national health, prosperity, and welfare; and to secure the national defense."[14] DARPA, established in 1958, is the central research and development organization for the Department of Defense.[15] As government agencies go, these are not large. The NSF budget is currently under six billion dollars, and DARPA's is less than three billion dollars. These organizations fund research in areas that would not deliver a return on investment to private companies. In fact basic research is unreliable when it comes to a return on investment. When such research does yield promising results, it is not uncommon for the benefits to be realized only after many, many years. But these agency's grants have funded some bonanzas.

An example of a research success that took several decades began in 1967 when DARPA funded a network called ARPANET. The purpose was to allow high speed computers to link over a cable network and thus avoid use of expensive long-distance telephone lines. In those days computers were gigantic machines that resided in rooms, not on tables. As Paul Light points out, ARPANET was "a vibrant partnership between the federal government, university scientists, and private firms."[16] Light goes onto describe how an "internetting problem" was solved in 1973, and that by 1983 some four hundred computers were connected through separate regional networks. In 1986, NSF formed a high-speed network called NSFnet. It also funded an undergraduate at the University of Illinois named Marc Andreesen. That young man invented the browser and eventually went on to found Netscape in 1994. The development of the Internet as we know it took over twenty-five years to mature and just a few years to become ubiquitous. Might the Internet have developed in the private sector? Perhaps, but if it had, someone would be collecting royalties, and we would be paying and paying and paying.

While the freedom to make choices expanded over the twentieth century, several freedoms in the area of commerce were reduced. These were the freedoms to deal dishonestly and to market unsafe products. Public investment in the regulation of commerce was not a new idea. The requirement that weights and measures be accurate has been around for centuries. According to a biblical verse, "You shall do no unrighteousness in judgment, in length, in weight, or in measure."[17] Inspection of scales and gasoline pumps is a government function we now take for granted. In 1906, our legislators passed the first of many laws protecting buyers from unsafe and dishonestly marketed products. The Food and Drug Act of that year required food and drugs to be properly labeled and gave the government authority to inspect food processing plants. In the same year Congress passed the Federal Meat Inspection Act. Credit for the passage of these Acts is given to a novel, *The Jungle*, Upton Sinclair's exposé of conditions in slaughter houses. Gradually food and drug laws were strengthened. For example, poultry inspection began in the 1920s but was strengthened in the 1950s. A law requiring pesticides to be registered with the Department of Agriculture was passed in 1947. The banning of DDT and other pesticides that persist in the environment did not take place until the early 1970s.

It took a substantial campaign led over several years by Ralph Nader to exclude unsafe automobiles and other consumer items from the marketplace. Nader's book *Unsafe at Any Speed* helped build support for legislation. Others weighed in as well, including *Consumer Reports*, which found a decline in the quality standards in automobiles between 1955 and 1965. In 1966, 26 automobile safety standards were mandated by Congress, including collapsible steering columns, safety glass and glazing materials (already used in European vehicles), air pollution control devices, anchors for seat belts, and recessed instrument panels. Passive restraints (air bags) were not required until 1989.[18]

The mandate of the Consumer Product Safety Commission, formed in 1972, is to protect the public "from unreasonable risks of serious injury or death from more than 15,000 types of consumer products under the agency's jurisdiction."[19] The Commission claims to have "contributed significantly to the 30 percent decline in the rate of deaths and injuries associated with consumer products over the past 30 years."

Unlike scale accuracy, food, drug, and product safety can be controversial. No one argues about excluding cattle with mad cow disease from the marketplace, but there has been disagreement about how extensively the government should inspect cattle to exclude the disease. Controversy about drug safety seems to go on continuously for reasons that are understandable. A great deal of time and money is expended to test a new drug or medical device. Testing of these products follows protocols dictated and audited by the Food and Drug Administration. Most of us prefer to take medication whose risks are known to be very low. But someone who is seriously ill might prefer to bear a greater risk with a new drug if alternatives have been exhausted.

In the absence of protocols to test products, safety can be subjective. While most approve of government regulation of safety, Democrats and liberals prefer more protection for buyers, while Republicans, libertarians, and others on the right prefer to give businesses more latitude.

When the business is a public company, not only must its products be safe but its securities must also be truthfully described. Regulation of securities, like that of some other products, came after a disaster. The Securities and Exchange Commission's (SEC) website describes the circumstances leading to its creation in 1934.[20]

> During the 1920s, approximately 20 million large and small shareholders took advantage of post-war prosperity and set out to make their fortunes in the stock market. It is estimated that of the $50 billion in new securities offered during this period, *half* became worthless. When the stock market crashed in October 1929, the fortunes of

countless investors were lost. Banks also lost great sums of money in the Crash because they had invested heavily in the markets (italics added).

The primary mission of the SEC is "to protect investors and maintain the integrity of the securities markets." The laws which the SEC enforces require public companies to be truthful about their businesses, their securities, and the risk an investor assumes when investing in their company. They also require brokers, dealers, and exchanges to "treat investors fairly and honestly, putting investors' interests first."[21]

Although the vast majority of public companies abide by SEC regulations, regulation occasionally fails and sometimes badly. The SEC did not catch Enron before it collapsed in 2001. Why? While systematic problems regarding auditor independence were uncovered, SEC under-funding and under-staffing might also have been a factor. In 2000 the Commission complained of serious staff attrition. Compensation for professionals was lower than that for comparable positions at other regulatory agencies and in the private sector.[22] According to a newspaper editorial about the SEC budget in 2003,[23]

> Tales of SEC under funding are legendary. Employee turnover was at a high of 35 percent during the bull market, in no small part because salaries for SEC lawyers are a pittance compared to those of their corporate counterparts. Between 1993 and 2001, the number of public companies skyrocketed and stock market trading volume went up six fold. Yet the agency's enforcement staff grew by just 15 percent. As a result, SEC investigators are able to review only a tiny fraction of all corporate filings, routinely leaving thousands of financial reports unchecked. Investigations are cut short for lack of resources.

Funding for the SEC since the Enron scandal has increased substantially. Whether it might catch another Enron is impossible to say, but it appears that the odds of it succeeding are improving.

In contrast to the topics covered so far in this chapter, the subject of health and life expectancy does not seem related to the concept of freedom in an obvious way. However, there is a relationship. Life expectancy in 1900 was less than fifty years,[24] which means, as noted earlier, that a majority of Americans didn't live long enough to retire. An early death and a much greater prevalence of disease robbed Americans of choices we take for granted today (when life expectancy is over seventy-five years[25]). Conservatives will want to attribute some of the improvement in health and life expectancy to the improved diet and shelter we enjoy with our prosperity, and they are right. But just because there is enough to eat doesn't automatically assure that children and adults will understand what it takes to be well nourished. And the pathogens conquered in the last century and the insights we now have on major killers such as heart disease and cancer do not follow from prosperity. Polio, for example, struck children and some adults regardless of their economic status. Franklin Delano Roosevelt, member of a patrician, New York family, was its most famous victim.

Today we are accustomed to taking such medical progress for granted as we struggle with the increasing costs of health care. Many childhood diseases (some of which could also affect adults) and their possible complications have been largely forgotten. They could be devastating. Thousands, including one American president would never again walk unassisted after contracting polio. Some were condemned to spend the remainder of their lives in iron lungs. Most of those affected were children. German measles, by contrast, usually was a pretty easy illness to tolerate, but those who contracted it during pregnancy risked having a child with congenital defects. Measles could cause serious respiratory complications, and one in one thousand of those infected with this disease contracted encephalitis. Mortality from this complication was between 10 percent and 30 percent, and another 40 percent had permanent neurological effects.

That diseases such as polio, German measles and whooping cough are either distant memories or unknown to most Americans testifies to the success of government vaccination programs. These programs, which began in the 1950s, along with the introduction of antibiotics in the 1940s, have led to a substantial reduction in communicable and infectious diseases. We still have some very dangerous diseases such as AIDS and SARS to deal with, but the list of dangerous diseases that no longer pose a threat is very long. The agency that detects the development and cause of disease is the Center for Disease Control (CDC) in Atlanta. Among its successes was finding the cause for Legionnaires disease, Reye's Syndrome, and hantavirus pulmonary syndrome. In addition to epidemiological and disease detective work, CDC has participated in eradication and control efforts. In the 1960s it helped vaccinate Africans against smallpox in 20 countries which contributed to the eventual worldwide abolition of this disease.

The major government organizations dedicated to medical research are the National Institutes of Health (NIH). Headquartered in Bethesda, Maryland, the NIH is composed of 27 institutes and centers, each dedicated to a disease or group of diseases. NIH has contributed grants to over 100 Nobel laureates, including seven of its own scientists. NIH spends most of our tax dollars on grants to over 2,000 institutions in the United States and abroad. One of NIH's best known projects is the Framingham (Massachusetts) Heart Study, now over 50 years old, which has played an important role in identifying the risk factors for heart disease such as elevated cholesterol, high blood pressure, smoking, faulty diet, and a sedentary life style. In 1971 the study was extended to a second generation which will enable scientists to look at genetic factors in heart disease and obesity, diabetes, and Alzheimer's disease. More recently, minority residents of Framingham were recruited to participate.

NIH-supported research has played a major role in improving health and preventing premature death in a number of areas. For example, between 1977 and 1999 death from heart disease, the nation's number one killer, dropped by 36 percent, and during the same period death from stroke declined by 50 percent.[26]

Besides avoiding significant suffering, prevention of disease led to substantial savings in health costs. "Every dollar spent immunizing children against measles, mumps and rubella saves $21 in future health costs, for example, while every dollar spent on vaccinations for diphtheria-pertussis-tetanus (DPT) saves $29."[27] Vaccination programs provide a modern example of the old nostrum that an ounce of prevention is worth a pound of cure.

A modern way to express avoiding future costs is to call it a return on investment: the return is the medical costs prevented, and the investment is the cost of the vaccination program. Return on investment has been calculated not only for health costs, but also for social costs. For example, one could calculate the savings to society of a rehabilitation program that prevents prison inmates from re-offending or a program that helps substance abusers overcome their addictions. Of course we need to know what proportion of these populations is helped by such programs in order to compute an acceptable value.

A return on investment for early childhood education has been calculated by the Senior Vice President and Director of the Federal Reserve Bank of Minneapolis, Art Rolnick.[28] Programs for young children that reduce the likelihood of future problems should have the greatest claim on our attention. Head Start and programs like it have been functioning since the 1960s, and by this time a number of studies on them have been completed. Children who enrolled in Head Start or other similar programs benefit in a number of ways: While enrolled they receive good quality child care; after completing the program they tend to do better in school and tend to earn more as adults. Society benefits in a number of ways as well: It spends less on welfare payments, adult education services, and crime. Rolnick and Grunewald calculated the return on investment to society for Head Start or programs like it as 12 percent and to the individual who attends as 4 percent, for a total of 16 percent. He points out that this return on investment is considerably greater than that of most private investments.

The importance of government to our daily lives in ways most of us approve can be deduced from the quality of life we desire. A way to determine this is to ask what factors do we consider when we choose a place to live, and how does government affect these? Conservatives and liberals often disagree about how rigorously a government regulation should be enforced, but agree that there should be a regulation. For example the two sides disagree about how the Clean Air Act should be enforced, but everyone wants to live in a place where the air is clean. And everyone understands that clean air depends not only on one's own residential area, but also on air pollution from sources hundreds of miles away. So a way to extract our consensus from our political disagreements is to consider where people prefer to live.

References devoted to the subject of choosing and rating a place to live provide a list of factors that maximize quality of life.[29] Certainly the most important is the opportunity for employment. Would government activity make employment more likely? It's hard to see a relationship over the period of a few years. Comparing the top ten in state and local taxes as a percent of personal income to the top ten in growth between 1997 and 2001 we find New York and Vermont in the top ten of both lists. However, comparing the bottom ten in state and local taxes as a percent of personal income to the bottom ten in growth between 1997 and 2001 we find North Carolina, Missouri, Florida and Nevada on both lists. High taxed Hawaii had a low growth rate between 1997 and 2001, and low taxed New Hampshire and South Dakota had top ten growth rates for the same period.[30] Over the long haul, however, states that invest in human and physical infrastructure can be expected to have an advantage.

Government investment is not likely to have any effect on climate. Cost-of-living is a factor that does include tax rates, but also other costs such as housing, food, and health care. Government could have a small effect in this factor. Government plays a larger role in the next factor, education. In addition to primary and secondary education, some 80 percent of colleges or universities are supported by tax dollars, most of it coming from state coffers.

The public sector is also involved in the area of crime. Of course, some choose an area to live because it is low in crime. New affluent suburbanites might not attribute low crime rates to their police departments, but they would have to agree that keeping crime low ultimately depends on their police force.

By contrast, the place of the public sector in supporting recreation and the arts is clear: Tax dollars make a contribution. The for-profit and nonprofit sectors support sports, night clubs, movie theaters, restaurants, art museums, symphony orchestras, and dance companies, while the public sector supports libraries and recreation areas such as parks, hiking and bike trails, swimming facilities, some golf courses, and zoos.

The public sector contributes to the quality of health care directly by supporting some health care facilities and indirectly by educating health care professionals, maintaining public health, and funding clinical research. The importance of government in maintaining clean water and air was alluded to earlier. Some conservatives like to remind Americans about just how clean our air and water has become. They say that the other side complains too much. They follow the sentiment if not the words of Ronald Reagan who infamously and mistakenly likened air pollution to the natural emissions of the Smoky Mountains.

The American Lung Association's most recent report confirms the concern of those in the liberal camp.[31] "High levels of microscopic, soot-like particles are increasing the risk of premature death for millions of people, including those with heart or lung disease." The American Lung Association's State of the Air: 2004 report continues, "While particle pollution emerges as a widespread problem affecting a quarter of all Americans, ozone levels continue to endanger nearly half the nation (136 million Americans)."

The following table summarizes the government's effect on the factors we have considered in a place to live.

Table 4.1
Government's Role in Quality of Life

Factor affecting quality of life	Government effect
Air quality	Positive
Water quality	Positive
Climate	No effect
Economic opportunity	Positive long term, neutral short term
Cost of living	Somewhat negative
Education	Positive
Crime	Positive
Recreation	Somewhat positive
Health care	Somewhat positive

Social Security and Medicare are programs to which we contribute and which have enjoyed broad public acceptance. For example, in

2000 the Gallup Poll found wide agreement on the importance of Social Security: 74 percent of young people (18 to 29 years old) found it important or extremely important as did 93 percent of Americans 65 years and over. Intermediate ages had opinions in between the percentages quoted.[32] Conservatives don't propose doing away with them, but they have suggestions on making what they consider improvements. They have been raising alarms about Social Security for so long that many believe the system is in imminent danger. More to their point, increasing numbers of citizens believe they will not be able to count on it when they retire. In 2004 the Social Security trustees who oversee the Social Security Trust Fund reported that it will be exhausted in the year 2042 and that after that it would be able to pay only 75 percent of promised benefits. The problem we have is a result of borrowing from the Trust Fund and the uncertainty—given the budget deficit—whether those borrowed funds can be restored.

Finally, the government we have elected has taken on projects which may not have been absolutely necessary but were and are widely acceptable to most Americans. They have not affected our freedom in any obvious way, but it's likely that most citizens do not begrudge the tax revenues that supported them. For example, we had to compete in the space race, but we really didn't have to go to the moon. The Russians had beat us to space with Sputnik in 1957, put the first animal into space in 1959, and then put the first man in space in 1961. Our first astronaut, John Glenn, didn't get into orbit until 1962.

We achieved the goal set by President Kennedy in 1961 of landing a man on the moon and bringing him back safely in 1969. We continue to lead the world in space exploration with projects such as the Hubble Space Telescope and the robots sent to Mars. The vast majority of benefits to today's space projects are to the basic sciences, but we all can share in the excitement when little remotely operated robots roll around the red planet, take pictures, and analyze samples, and when the Hubble telescope sends back photos of hundreds of galaxies never before imagined.

Long before our space program began, we undertook a four-year project aimed to help our allies and enemies after World War II. The idea came out of a State Department group chartered by a new Secretary of State, George C. Marshall, formerly chief of staff of the Army during the War. Marshall announced the plan in a short commencement speech at Harvard University in 1947. In that speech he said, "The breakdown of the business structure of Europe during the war was complete . . . The truth of the matter is that Europe's requirements for the next three or four years of foreign food and other essential products—principally from America—are so much greater than her present ability to pay that she must have substantial additional help or face economic, social, and political deterioration of a very grave character."[33]

Justification for what would come to be called the Marshall Plan came from several considerations. "Our policy is directed not against any country or doctrine but against hunger, poverty, desperation and chaos," Marshall said. In that sentence he pointed both to a humanitarian motive and to a policy to ensure European and ultimately American security. A lesson from the previous world war had been learned. As Secretary of State Madelaine Albright noted at the same venue and occasion fifty years later, "After World War I, America had withdrawn from the world, shunning responsibility and avoiding risk. Others did the same. The result in the heart of Europe was the rise of great evil."[34] Most understood that the devastation after World War Two created conditions for new tyrannies. Most feared communism. The plan would also help to develop markets for U.S. businesses that had come through the war unscathed.

"The program," said Marshall, "should be a joint one, agreed to by a number, if not all European nations." Indeed all were invited, Allies and former enemies. The Soviet Union declined. The insistence on cooperation of recipients in planning the grants and its finite character of four years, were likely to have been significant for the plan's success. Congressional opposition to the plan dissolved after communists took over Czechoslovakia in 1948. It cost the United States twelve billion dollars (in 1948-year dollars), and the Plan was a smashing success. In recognition of its impact, America's soldier turned statesman Marshall received the Nobel Peace Prize in 1953.

A long time before the world wars, the U.S. government began to set aside land for parks, monuments and historic sites. That tradition was expanded during the twentieth century to include forests, wilderness areas, wild rivers, and shores. It began in 1864 when the Yosemite Valley was given by Congress to the State of California to preserve as a state park (it was later given back to the federal government). In 1872 Congress set aside a portion of the Wyoming and Montana territories as the first national park, Yellowstone. Others followed. "The idealistic impulse to preserve nature was often joined by the pragmatic desire to promote tourism: western railroads lobbied for many of the early parks and built grand rustic hotels in them to boost their passenger business."[35] In addition to preservation of sites of natural beauty, interest in historic places began in 1889 with protection of the prehistoric Indian ruins and artifacts at Arizona's Casa Grande Ruin.

The National Park Service (NPS), formed in 1916, has overseen the expansion of national parks, historic sites, and recreational areas. Education and restoration have become an important part of the NPS's work. During the great Depression of the 1930s it supervised the Civilian Conservation Corps (CCC) which put to work thousands of unemployed young men doing conservation, repair, and construction in both national and state parks. Their handiwork endures.

From the rugged coastline of Acadia to the dramatic canyons of Zion National Park in Utah, Americans flock to the National Parks. In fiscal year 2000 (October 1, 1999 – September 30, 2000) approximately 290 million people visited them. That is slightly more than once for each man, woman, and child in the United States (the population in that year was 281 million). NPS also manages the new World War Two Memorial in Washington D.C. along with the other memorials of that war and of our other wars.

We all agree that government should defend us against enemies foreign and domestic, provide a safe environment, and enforce the law. I argue for the value of government in additional roles: Our public investments provide us with increased individual choice, expanded business opportunities, increased scientific and technological ideas for our entrepreneurs to exploit, improved health, and an improved quality of life.

Conservatives claim that the private sector could accomplish some of the above even better. Could they? That is the subject of the next chapter.

CHAPTER FIVE

Myths of Government and Business

Today when job seekers are frustrated, they complain to friends and family but rarely do anything more drastic. In 1883 Charles Guiteau, angry and disappointed after repeatedly seeking a government post, went way beyond complaining. He assassinated the twentieth President of the United States, James A. Garfield. Very soon after that shocking event, Garfield's successor, Chester A. Arthur, signed into law the Pendleton Act, which set up the Civil Service Commission. Government jobs, which had been handed out by office holders to their supporters, were henceforth to be obtained by merit.

The Pendleton Act spelled the end of the spoils system at the national level. No longer would politicians be able to reward their friends with government jobs, at least not many of them. Elected officials had liked the spoils system. It allowed them to reward supporters. And those beholden to politicians could be relied upon to devote time and money to upcoming campaigns. But to some politicians, it had become a burden. President Garfield had found office-seekers "lying in wait" for him "like vultures for a wounded bison."[1]

Over many years, the solution to the spoils system began to look as if it were becoming a problem itself. To many citizens, civil servants seemed rigid, unresponsive and prone to waste our tax dollars. By 1976, Jimmy Carter ran a successful presidential campaign in which opposition to the bureaucracy played a prominent part. His campaign brochure asserted, "We can no longer drift along with a complicated, confused overlapping and wasteful bureaucracy."[2] President Reagan also ran against Washington and was far more critical. In his speech, "To Restore America," he said, "The Washington Establishment is not the answer. It's the problem."[3] And part of the problem for these presidents and many private citizens was the Civil Service. In contrast to Carter, Reagan and many of his followers were and are confident that the private sector can do what government does only better and more cheaply.

If the Civil Service were the problem that presidents and other citizens allege, then government in Washington should have been getting better for several decades, because the Civil Service in absolute and percentage terms has been getting smaller and smaller. Federal civil servants numbered fewer than 1.8 million in 2002. In the same year a study of the size of government conducted by Paul Light[4] showed that the federal government employed just over eight million contractors and grant recipients. These private sector employees are "off the books," and their function, location and salary are not subject to public scrutiny. Along with nearly 1.5 million uniformed personnel and 875,000 postal service employees, the true size of government, according to the study, was over twelve million. That overall total declined during the 1990s, partly because the Cold War ended.

But the reduction in size has stopped. The war on terrorism is one reason, but other departments of government including Health and Human Services have hired additional workers. Light writes that "The 2002 true size of government is still smaller than it was at the end of the Cold War in 1990, but is only smaller because of a reduction of nearly one million civil service and uniformed military jobs over the 1990s, almost all of which were cut at the Departments of Defense and Energy, and the National Aeronautics and Space Administration." Of some consolation to the manufacturing sector, manufacturing jobs accounted "for the largest increase in the contract workforce."[5] That is mainly because of defense spending for weapon systems.

Even though civil servants comprise only 14 percent of the Federal work force, conservatives still maintain that government agencies are inefficient, wasteful, and unresponsive. Could the private sector do it better?

There are a few government agencies which function similarly enough to the private sector to allow comparison. Two agencies, the Social Security Administration (SSA) and Medicare, the two largest social welfare agencies in the Federal government, are noteworthy.

Most agree that the SSA's administrative costs, 0.6 percent of total expenditures,[6] are lower than comparable costs in the private sector. Critics of the current social security system generally agree that alternative plans are likely to cost somewhat more to administer.[7] The likelihood of higher costs and higher yields—and therefore higher risks—associated with various alternative proposals to the current system have been widely discussed and will not be explored here.

Recipients of SSA benefits are quite satisfied with the service they receive. The American Customer Satisfaction Index (ACSI), produced by a partnership of the University of Michigan Business School and the American Society of Quality, has been measuring consumer experiences with products and services since 1994.[8] Benefit recipients recently gave the SSA a score of 81.[9] That rating compared well with a rating of 77 from customers of life insurance companies, 78 from customers of property and casualty insurance companies, and 75 for banking customers.[10]

Satisfaction scores can be influenced by customer expectations, and it is possible that lower expectations played a part in the score the SSA received. Professor Claes Fornell of the University of Michigan Business School suggests several reasons. Expectations can be raised by advertising and public agencies don't advertise. Also, many citizens are first time users who don't know what to expect of an agency and who have low expectations of government services. Subsequent experience changes their view. "There seems to be a difference," the professor writes, "between the public opinion of government and the actual satisfaction by the users of government agencies."[11]

Medicare also compares favorably to the private sector. Medicare's administrative costs, a few percent of premiums received, are much less than private insurance companies' overhead. Also, the ACSI satisfaction score of 77 for Medicare recipients is higher than the score of 70 for private health insurance customers.[12] Lower administrative costs mean that more dollars go to health care and less to administer the system. Even the Canadian national insurance program costs less to administer than our private health insurance companies. Authors of a study published in the prestigious *New England Journal of Medicine* found that in 1999 the Canadian program's administrative costs were 1.3 percent compared to the overhead of 11.7 percent for private insurers in the United States, 3.6 percent for Medicare and 6.8 percent for Medicaid.[13] According to the authors' calculations the cost to administer health care for U.S. citizens is $1,059 per capita compared with $307 per capita for Canadian citizens. That difference amounts to a total of $209 billion.[14] That's money that we spend on health care administrative expenses that Canadians would spend on health care. US health care is the costliest in the world, and high administrative expense is one of the reasons.

These public-to-private comparisons cast doubt on the widely assumed superiority of the private sector efficiency, productivity, and customer service. Many private organizations are efficient and productive, but if that desired state were so common we would not hear stories of dramatic recoveries and improvements quite so often. Stories about two widely admired American companies illustrate this point.

In an interview broadcast over a decade ago, David Kearns, Chief

Executive Officer (CEO) of Xerox in 1982, recalled how his company became aware that Japanese copiers were sold in retail stores for less than it cost Xerox to manufacture them. Adding the cost of distribution further widened the cost gap between the Xerox and Japanese products. He also knew that his Japanese competitors were getting new products to market in half the time it took Xerox.[15] He admitted to doubts at the time about whether Xerox could continue to survive.

About the same time that Xerox learned of Japan's superior efficiency in design and manufacture of copy machines, U.S. auto manufacturers were also feeling threatened. In 1980 Japan produced 11 million automobiles, surpassing the number produced by U.S. companies for the first time. The Japanese had improved their production processes and consequently their products, by using principles learned from American quality innovators W. Edward Deming and Joseph Juran and Japanese quality experts such as Kaoru Ishikawa and Genichi Taguchi. Their ideas, collectively called the Quality Movement, included many that are now taken for granted in the business world:

- Customer requirements and customer satisfaction must always be at the center of a company's concern.
- Improve a product or service by improving the process that creates it, or create a better process.
- Employees must be included in process improvement, because they know the processes they use better than their managers do.
- Employee groups brought together in teams are the agent for improvement.
- Management must be committed to process improvement and must provide strategic planning for quality.
- To improve processes, variation must be reduced; process variation is the enemy of product (and service) quality.

- To improve anything, one must be able to measure it; to measure the reduction in variation, use statistical process control.
- The process improvement procedure is an application of scientific method.

Xerox regained the market share it lost to the Japanese by introducing a new quality program in the early 1980s. The program, adapted from several quality gurus of the time, included a nine-step improvement process that identified and then achieved customers' requirements. The process used problem solving and statistical tools, competitive benchmarking, indicators to measure progress and customer satisfaction, and an assessment of the cost of the lack of quality.[16] Xerox won the Malcolm Baldridge National Quality Award in 1989, an annual honor awarded by the U.S. President to organizations with demonstrated commitment to quality practices and performance excellence.[17]

Despite regaining its market share, becoming an efficient organization, and winning the Baldridge Award, Xerox was not able to celebrate for very long. Between 1993 and 1995, the company laid off 12,000 (out of 97,000) employees. Then serious problems developed in 1999 with two simultaneous initiatives: consolidation of its administrative centers and reorganization of its sales division. The billing system was thrown into disarray. Errors in orders and price quotes showed up, and some of these took months to resolve. Long-term customers left.

Xerox tried to fix the problems itself, but eventually turned to General Electric (GE) Capital for help. GE helped fix the billing problems and introduced Xerox to a method of diagnosing and fixing problems much more quickly and effectively than anything they had known. But Xerox faced other problems as well: a downturn in demand for their products, fierce competition, and accounting problems. The company had to sell assets, cut costs, and concentrate on development of its core businesses. True to its tradition of innovation, Xerox developed new products and services which proved to be a success in the marketplace.

As Xerox recovered its bearings in 2002, it began training its executives in a variation of Lean Six Sigma, the method it learned from GE. Xerox realized dramatic results. In 2003, Xerox claimed to achieve a $6 million return on a $14 million investment in Lean Six Sigma.[18] And as GE had used this method to help its customers, Xerox started to use it help its customers succeed.

GE learned about Six Sigma from its creator, Motorola Corporation. This method starts with the ideas of the Quality Movement of the 1980s and, in GE's version, adds these requirements:

- Top executives must be committed to the process
- Extensive training of managers and employees is necessary— usually one week for practitioners to one month for leaders (called Black Belts)
- Processes to be repaired must be measured before and after improvement.
- Labor and materials used to effect an improvement are closely monitored.
- From these measurements, a return on investment for each project is calculated.
- Six Sigma makes extensive use of statistical tools.

The name Six Sigma refers to the number of defects, 3.4 per million, that the method attempts to attain. GE defines a defect as a failure to deliver what a customer wants. Traditional quality methods aimed for three sigma, or 66,800 defects per million. GE learned, as had Motorola before it, that three sigma was not good enough for their customers.

Lean Six Sigma adds features to Six Sigma that were developed by Toyota in the 1980s for reducing waste. Lean Manufacturing (sometimes called simply Lean) adds several ideas:

- Keep needed tools within easy reach
- Introduce error-proof processes
- Be sure gauges used are easy to read
- Allow workers to stop production if a problem occurs
- Continuously improve
- Emphasize that creativity is more important than capital

Jack Welch embarked on Six Sigma with GE in 1995. He had already introduced other improvement initiatives after becoming head of the GE in 1981. First he sold businesses that did not measure up to his standards and bought others that did. He then reduced GE's workforce from 412,000 to 229,000. A program in the 1980s encouraged "boundaryless" behavior in which everyone could contribute ideas. Bureaucracy was to be "decimated."[19] Welch continuously worked for improvement. "No one in American business had the vision," writes Robert Slater,[20] "to fix something that wasn't broken." Welch believes in change and that "GE can only suffer if it stands still." In his letter to stockholders in GE's 1998 Annual Report he wrote, ". . . . we plunged into Six Sigma with a Company-consuming vengeance just over three years ago. We have invested more than a billion dollars in the effort, and the financial returns have now entered the exponential phase—more than three quarters of a billion dollars in savings beyond our investment in 1998, with a billion and a half in sight for 1999."[21] GE later reported that Six Sigma saved it $2 billion in 1999.

After pursuing cost reduction and high efficiency inside the company for several years, GE turned outward to help its customers succeed. In his letter to share owners in 2000 he wrote, "GE completed more than 2000 Six Sigma projects 'at the customer, for the customer,' last year. Here we took GE resources and applied them to our customers' biggest needs, using Six Sigma as a foundation."[22]

Under Jack Welch, GE achieved high efficiency, and Xerox, led by Ann Mulcahy, appears to be doing the same. I have not dealt with the challenges these companies faced from competition and the whims of the economy. Nor do I want to suggest that these companies' improvements using quality techniques are more important than the products and services they offer their customers. The examples of GE and Xerox do illustrate that a highly productive and efficient organization is not a natural or normal state in the private sector. It requires incessant (Jack Welch would probably say "fanatic") effort on the part of management to gain and maintain such efficiency. Xerox achieved that state in 1989, lost it a few years later and appears to be gaining it again.

High efficiency and productivity require consistent leadership, a large investment in training and information technology, and a permanent change in an organization's culture. That last-mentioned factor is the most difficult. The pithy comment "culture eats strategic plans for lunch,"[23] may understate the issue. Constantly striving to improve is not a natural or comfortable way to behave. To continue to improve one must continue to admit that one's current way of doing things is not the best.

GE's assistance to Xerox in resolving billing problems was described earlier. Xerox continued to use GE for its billing processes. In other words, Xerox outsourced its billing to GE. Offshore outsourcing, sending jobs abroad, has received bad press in recent years, but "onshore" outsourcing is much more common and has become increasingly popular among U.S. businesses since the early 1990s. Conservatives maintain that governments save money by outsourcing tasks.

Before discussing outsourcing a few definitions are appropriate. Outsourcing is a type of service. In the public sector it is sometimes called "privatizing." Outsourcing is a type of contracting that involves a business process, not just a skill or project. Early outsourcing was used almost entirely for information technology (IT) processes. IT refers to all the hardware (personal computers, printers, scanners, servers, networks, firewalls, cables etc.) and software that a majority of us now use in the workplace. Some companies outsource their entire IT processes, but most outsource a portion, such as the help desk, network support or email management. Outsourcing has grown and now includes portions of human resource functions, accounting, training, maintenance, physical security, legal tasks, and research. Government has outsourced the same functions as the private sector as well as traditionally public tasks including various military processes, prisons, day-to-day operation of the space shuttle and welfare administration.

Why outsource? Companies outsource for one or more of the following reasons: to reduce costs, to free up resources (human and capital) so that processes that are essential to an organization's mission can be better served (this is usually referred to as focusing on one's core business), to provide performance superior to that which can be done by a company's own personnel, to gain expertise that can be relied upon to perform as promised, and to successfully adapt to changing technological requirements and opportunities. Organizations also use outsourcing and contracting to temporarily (days to years) increase an organization's staff.

Outsourcing is related to organizational efficiency, the topic discussed above. In order for an outsourcer to save costs for a customer, it must be able to perform the job more efficiently than the customer. Its operating costs, other costs (administration, marketing, etc) and its desired profit margin must add up to less than the customer's current cost.

The Defense Department is using outsourcing and contracting to increase its workforce during the Iraqi war to a degree not seen before. Estimates suggest that one in ten Americans in Iraq is a contractor. But the outsourcing of government functions to the private sector did not start during the Bush administration, and it is not limited to the U.S. government. It is one manifestation of the administrative reform—a movement toward more business-like management methods in the public sector—that occurred in nations around the world in the last few decades of the twentieth century.

According to Accenture,[24] federal governments who outsource as much or more than the United States are Canada, Singapore, Hong Kong and Australia. Yet the world's "preeminent outsourcing government" is the United Kingdom (UK).[25] For example, in 1994 the UK's Inland Revenue (comparable to our Internal Revenue Service) outsourced its entire IT function for ten years to the US firm, EDS. In 2004 Cap Gemini Ernst and Young and its partner, Fujistu, replaced EDS in a contract valued at $5.5 billion for the next ten years. In contrast to the UK, according to the Accenture report, Australia has pulled back from its ambitious, centralized outsourcing and is instead implementing "second generation outsourcing," which appears to be comparatively limited and decentralized.

Do governments save money by outsourcing, as conservatives allege? A blanket answer cannot be given. Clearly they do sometimes. In the private sector, outsourcing's function as a cost saver has been uneven. Summarizing one of the results of a survey of IT executives co-sponsored by Getronics and CIO magazine in 2002, the authors wrote, "The main reason given for both increasing and decreasing outsourcing is cost reduction."[26] A research director at Gartner, Inc., a major IT consultancy, wrote in that organization's weblog, "When it comes to outsourcing, Gartner emphasizes that clients should not outsource to cut costs. If a client is not very cost-efficient, then the outsourcer may be able to reduce costs but that is not always the situation."[27] The clients here would be in the private sector. In the Accenture report cited above, half of the government leaders who outsourced to reduce costs were satisfied compared to much higher satisfaction percentages for those who outsourced for the kinds of reasons cited earlier. In the private sector human resource outsourcing (such as 401k administration, benefits management, training and recruitment) seems to result in cost reduction more consistently.

A survey of the 50 states conducted by The Council of State Governments (CSG) on the issue of outsourcing, here called privatization, reports:

> Most agency directors who responded to the CSG survey indicated that the extent of privatized services and programs remain relatively moderate, mostly less than 10 percent. Twelve budget directors said that their state has privatized on average, at least 6 percent of their services. Primary reasons for privatization include cost-savings, flexibility, lack of personnel and expertise and increased innovation. Most respondents reported savings from privatization to be between none to 5 percent. Nearly half the states said privatization is likely to increase and the other half said the extent of privatization is likely to remain the same.[28]

The savings these agency directors report is hardly a ringing endorsement of the conservative position.

A more recent example comes from the Office of Management and Budget (OMB), which reported on the results of 662 competitions between federal agencies and private bidders in the fiscal year 2003. In 89 percent of the assessments, the federal agency provided the best value. The costs of the competitions totaled $88 million, and OMB claims that replacing under 2,000 government employees will save $1.1 billion over three to five years.[29] The independent General Accounting Office (GAO) reported that in 2002, 75 percent of the sourcing competitions were won "in-house" by the government agencies.[30] These results do not bode well for conservative hopes of saving substantial amounts by handing off government work to the private sector.

Even with very little or no savings, public agencies are using IT outsourcing during periods of tight budgets. As explained in an article from *Governing*, "With tight budgets, most state and local agencies are limited in their ability to hire skilled IT staff or invest in high-tech equipment. Consequently, they are looking to the private sector for help in providing technology services. *They may not save money*, but for government budgeting purposes, it's easier to come up with revenue for an operational cost, such as a yearly service contract, than an appropriation for a large capital investment (Italics added)."[31] It is reasonable to expect that similar circumstances and responses occur at the federal level.

While outsourcing and contracting may solve dilemmas for public agencies, they also present problems. Since these costs are "off the books" it is very difficult to oversee this kind of activity. Even if there has been little evidence thus far of contracts being awarded as political favors, these would be difficult to detect. Contractors are not subject to the Hatch Act, which prevents civil servants from engaging in political activity.

Military outsourcing poses additional dilemmas. The insecure conditions in Iraq caused more than one contractor to pick up and leave as fast as their SUVs could carry them. The failure to show up worsens conditions for the armed forces. Though disruptive, this kind of problem is simple to understand.

Far more complex and troubling are other issues such as the hiring of intelligence services. Professor Debra Avant, whose forthcoming book will deal with the global market for military and security services, wrote, ". . . there are no standard procedures for deploying private security workers under military contracts, which makes it far more difficult to gather information about who they are, what they're doing and for whom. They are not part of the military command; they are not covered by the code of military justice."[32] The U.S. government's ability to hire private military forces gives more latitude to the executive branch to conduct covert operations without congressional oversight.

Conservatives argue that when those on public payrolls are inept or worse, they suffer no bad consequences because they are protected by their civil service or union status. What about those from the private sector who feed off the public trough? Some readers may remember reports years ago of $436 hammers and $7,600 coffeemakers. These were examples of "outrageously overpriced military spending" exposed over two decades ago by what is now known as the Project on Government Oversight (POGO). POGO's investigations suggest that the private sector does not suffer seriously when its work for the government is criminal or delinquent. Here is a summary of POGO's 2002 report, "Federal Contractor Misconduct: Failures of the Suspension and Debarment System:"

> Many of the U.S. government's largest contractors have been found to have repeatedly broken the law or engaged in misconduct, according to POGO's investigation. However, they are never even temporarily suspended, let alone debarred, from gaining additional government contracts, contrary to Reagan/Bush era laws. POGO's research found that, since 1990, 43 of the government's top contractors paid approximately $3.4 billion in fines/penalties, restitution, and settlements. Furthermore, four of the top 10 government contractors have at least two criminal convictions. And yet, only one of the top 43 contractors has been suspended or debarred from doing business with the government, and then, for only five days.[33]

This government watchdog recommended improvements in the procurement system that would prevent contractors with long "rap sheets" from receiving more tax dollars. Congress has yet to respond.

Some contractors receiving tax dollars are not paying taxes they owe to the IRS. The GAO reported in February of 2004 that over 27,000 contractors owed about $3 billion in unpaid taxes.[34] They also found "abusive or potentially criminal activity related to the federal tax system" in case studies of 47 Department of Defense contractors; most owed payroll taxes dating back to the early 1990s.

> One individual who owned a base support and custodial service borrowed over $1 million from his business. His company owes nearly $10 million in unpaid taxes and was paid over $40 million in DOD contract payments in one year. He bought several cars, a boat and a home in the Caribbean. In 2003 he dissolved his company and fled to the Caribbean where he is living today. In another case, an individual business that performs repair services on military vehicles owes over $500,000 in business and individual taxes. This contractor has contracts with DOD that are worth over $60 million and recently received an annual payment of over $100,000.[35]

It is not against the law for contractors behind in their tax payments to receive federal contracts.

Finally, since much maligning of the public sector has been anecdotal, it seems only fair to tell a few tales of for-profit organizations doing work formerly done by government. Both involve controversial areas of privatization, prisons and public schools.

You might think Wackenhut Corporation would have been extremely careful in managing their new juvenile detention center at Jena, Louisiana. This facility began taking in residents late in 1998 within weeks of a U.S. Department of Justice (DOJ) lawsuit alleging Louisiana's existing juvenile facilities—one of which was in private hands—were unsafe and lacked programs or services that juvenile prisoners required. Wackenhut was the largest private prison corporation in the world. Observers expected Wackenhut to have the expertise needed to run the new facility better than juvenile detention facilities already existing in Louisiana.

But much less than two years later, the U.S. DOJ was back in the courtroom of Federal District Court Judge Frank Polozola to add the Jena facility to its existing lawsuit. Among the Department's allegations were routine beating, vicious fights and rapes. Justice Department officials and others alleged that the problems at the facility were at least partly caused by Wackenhut's attempts to cut costs. Wackenhut officials claimed the charges were exaggerated, but what was known at the time about staffing suggested very serious problems. In a little over a year Jena had five different wardens. Employee turnover was very high. Wackenhut fired 125 employees "for either having sex with inmates, falsifying documents, using excessive force, bringing contraband to the prison or taking money, goods or favors from prisoners."[36]

Louisiana State Judge Mark Doherty revealed some of the effects of Wackenhut's staffing. After reading reports about the prison, Judge Doherty, a Republican and former prosecutor, went to Jena and interviewed inmates. Reports had found a one-fourth of the inmates to be "traumatically injured" in a two-month period.[37] Many had no shoes or jackets in the winter and "huddled under a shared sheet or blanket" to keep warm, rather than attend classes held in another building." A quarter of the inmates had I.Q.s under 70, but received no special education. Although it was built to treat young people with drug addictions, "virtually no drug treatment programs were run at Jena," according to the DOJ. Judge Doherty removed six teenage boys from Jena "after finding they had been brutalized by guards, kept in solitary confinement for months and deprived of shoes, blankets, education and medical care."[38] He found that instead of providing an opportunity for rehabilitation, inmates "wound up in a place that drives and treats juveniles as if they walked on all fours. These young people deserve to be treated like human beings, not animals."[39]

Bone-chilling cruelty occurred too. "A 15-year-old inmate from New Orleans also released by Judge Doherty tried to commit suicide 20 times by swallowing razor blades or hanging himself by a sheet. David

Utter, the inmate's lawyer, said Jena's files contained nearly two dozen reports that guards had used physical force against the teenager, causing a broken wrist and fingers." In perhaps the most egregious case of all, "Judge Doherty said one boy he released, a 17-year-old found guilty of robbery, had been forced to lie on the floor on his stomach with a guard's knee in his back, which caused excruciating pain since the boy had recently had an operation for gunshot wounds in his abdomen and was wearing a colostomy bag."[40]

The Jena facility was soon emptied of juveniles. As events played out Governor Foster said, "We won't be having any more private prisons in Louisiana as long as I'm governor."[41] In 2002, the Wackenhut Corporation, parent of the Wackenhut Corrections Corporation, was bought out by Group 4 Falck, a Danish security and prisons company. Wackenhut Corrections Corporation then bought its stake from its former parent. In 2003 it changed its name to The Geo Group. According to its website it operates prison facilities in thirteen states as well as Australia, New Zealand and South Africa.[42] In the US, it's been estimated that about 6 percent of the prison population are housed in private facilities (including the Geo Group facilities).[43]

For-profit prisons have generated criticism and controversy. So do for-profit schools. Before Chris Whittle founded Edison Schools, he had already made a fortune in communications of various kinds, including a partnership which successfully revived *Esquire* magazine in the early 1980s. A gifted salesman and entrepreneur, Whittle set his sights on public education in 1992. It would take special gifts to persuade others that a for-profit enterprise could educate children better than the public or non-profit sector. He believed he could do well while doing good. He maintained that if he could build enough schools (replacing failing schools), then he would benefit from economies of scale. One dubious educator said, "Their expectation of making profits by building on economies of scale is inconsistent with what we know about the production of education. The problem is that when you establish new schools, you have large variable costs."[44]

Whittle was unconvinced by doubting educators. He persuaded the President of Yale University, Benno Schmidt Jr., to join him in what he called the Edison Project.[45] He gave a group of education experts $50 million and two years to develop curriculum and a design. He leaned on his profitable enterprises too hard and had to lay off personnel and eventually sell those businesses. He was left with only the Edison Project. He and Schmidt obtained venture capital and gained their first opportunity in 1995 when the School Board in Wichita, Kansas hired Edison to take over two failing schools. It wasn't what Whittle had envisioned. He would not be able to build new schools. But the design his experts had created was implemented. It included a strong emphasis on reading, greater time for teacher training and preparation than is usually allotted, a software package that helped teachers understand individual students' learning needs, a longer school day, and a longer school year.

Using Edison methods, Whittle and his colleagues expanded and by 1998 were running schools in thirty cities. To continue to expand, Edison Schools needed more capital. Whittle took Edison Schools public during the bull market of the late 1990s. And he saw his first opportunity for profitability as part of the solution to widely publicized problems in the Philadelphia Public Schools. In 2002 the State of Pennsylvania had taken over the city's poorly performing schools and replaced the School Board with a School Reform Commission. Part of a five-year plan to improve the schools was to hire managers outside the school system. Whittle hoped to win management of as many as 60 or as few as 45 schools. He was awarded 20. That disappointment led to a collapse in the price of Edison's stock. In 2003 Whittle and Liberty Partners offered to buy out Edison stockholders for $1.76 a share. The buyout was sorely disappointing for stockholders who had bought the stock at issue for $18 per share and those who had paid as much as $38 per share. Yet since the stock had also sold under a dollar per share for a period of time, some saw a profit.

The Edison stockholder buyout attracted additional critics. Two months after the announcement to go private, Edison showed its first profit in its eleven year history. Whittle stood to gain $21 million from the buyout which some resented. Liberty Partners, who lent Whittle over a million dollars and assumed Edison's $74 million debt, "manages Florida's state pension funds, and union members and retirees said they were angry their pension funds were being used for what they considered a risky investment."[46]

Conservative advocates of privatizing schools cannot be pleased with Edison School's life as a public company, but are probably happy with developments in the Philadelphia schools. Happy, but not thrilled. When Edison was chosen to manage 20 schools, three other for-profit education management companies, two non-profit management companies, and two organizations from Temple University and the University of Pennsylvania were also chosen. Many schools remained under School District management. At the end of the second school year the *Philadelphia Inquirer* reported, "Philadelphia School District students scored better on standardized exams than they did last spring, and most regular district schools showed more improvement than those run by five of six outside managers."[47] Universal Companies, a non-profit which runs two schools and uses "the school district's curriculum, programs and overall model for reform," came in first among the privately managed schools. Edison came in second. The other non-profit showed the least improvement (one for-profit group was eliminated early on.)

Additional testing and the experience of several more years are needed before any conclusions about Philadelphia's educational competition can be made. Keep in mind that unlike public companies, private for-profit companies can function and even grow indefinitely without being profitable. If nothing is left over after staff is paid, physical plant maintained, necessary capital expenditures purchased and research and development continued, a company can continue to do business. However Edison, which has had both successes and failures outside of Philadelphia[48], will need to justify the investment made by the Florida's state pension funds.

In response to the right's claim that government is more expensive and less efficient than the for-profit sector, this chapter has offered the following:

- Two of the largest agencies of the U.S. government, the Social Security Administration (SSA) and the Centers for Medicare and Medicaid Services, which administer Medicare and Medicaid have more efficient administrations than do comparable private organizations. Two of them, SSA and Medicare, also receive higher scores on customer satisfaction than comparable private organizations.
- Private organizations are not always very efficient. It takes strong executive leadership to make and keep a business efficient. It doesn't just happen because an organization is profitable.
- Outsourcing provides several advantages to business and government. As a cost saver for government, its role appears to be limited.
- The right's claim that the private sector would be more accountable to the citizenry than government agencies is given the lie by the dismal record of the government continuing to hire contractors who have repeatedly broken the law or engaged in misconduct. To that list of those offenders, contractors in serious tax arrears must be added.

CHAPTER SIX

On Charity and Faith

Are you willing to use your checkbook to contribute your share of what is required to care for those in need in this country? Do you think everyone else might? What if they don't? Are you prepared to entrust care of the vulnerable in our society to the best efforts of volunteers and charitable organizations?

Conservatives would like charity to be voluntary. Some suggest that in our affluent society we can change our tax laws to encourage charitable giving and enlist civic organizations and groups fired by faith to care for those in need. Conservatives assert that charitable organizations significantly aided the disadvantages in the past.[1] If our forebears could do it, why can't we?

It is true that in earlier times voluntary contributions were an important source of funds to support what was called the "deserving poor." But it is also true that government has been involved for a very long time. As far back as the sixteenth century, the government of England was requiring those with means to help those in need. Early in this country's history, following English precedent, both private and public support served those who were unable to care for themselves. It is also true that government support was deployed at the local level and that, except for the substantial expenditure for pensions to Civil War veterans who fought for the union, national government was not a significant factor in what we now call welfare. Private charitable organizations played a significant role in caring for the poor during the later nineteenth and early twentieth centuries. The profession of social work was born and developed within these private institutions.

It was to those charitable organizations, as well as foundations and corporations, that President Hoover looked for help in bringing this country out of a developing economic depression that began in 1929. Hoover had earlier earned a national reputation as the brilliant administrator of relief to millions of hungry and poorly clothed European civilians during World War One. Governments provided a significant portion of the funds for that relief as grants and loans. The U.S. government donated the most.[2] After the war Hoover continued to administer relief funds especially to sick and undernourished European children. One of his last projects was for famine relief for the Russian Socialist Federated Soviet Republic. Congress allocated $24 million which was supposed to be partially reimbursed by the Bolshevik government with $12 million in gold. The Bolsheviks, swallowing their philosophical opposition to philanthropy, accepted[3]

But when the Great Depression began—its magnitude not yet appreciated—Hoover looked to the private sector to help the nation get back on its feet. He was adamant about preventing the U.S. from becoming a welfare state like Britain or Germany. The Federal government would serve only as facilitator, information provider, and cheerleader. But the economic malaise continued and worsened. The Hoover administration's initiatives were too little and too late. Existing private and public organizations, both state and local were overwhelmed. The nation opted for change. Under the next president, Franklin D. Roosevelt, the federal government inaugurated the New Deal, a group of programs to help the economically depressed.

Now, in a time of prosperity, many on the right want charity to return to the private sector. In order to decide if this proposal is reasonable, we first need to see how large a burden we would have to take on were government to stop writing the checks.

Table 6.1 summarizes the amount federal, state, and local government funds spent in 2000 on "income-tested" benefits.

Table 6.1
Cash and Noncash Benefits for Persons with Limited Income in the Year 2000[4]

Program	Amount (in billions)
Medical care	$225.8
Cash aid (including TANF and SSI)	$91.7
Food benefits (including food stamps, school lunches)	$34.3
Housing benefits	$34.9
Education (including Pell grants and Head Start)	$20.4
Services (including Title 20, child care, and block grants)	$20.7
Jobs and training	$7.3
Energy assistance	$1.7
TOTAL	**$437.0**

Nearly one-half of the amount spent on low-income citizens went to pay their medical bills. The federal government pays 70 percent of the total cash and non cash benefits of $437 billion, and state and local governments the remaining 30 percent.

The amount spent on the most widely discussed category of government aid, Temporary Assistance to Needy Families (TANF), the program that replaced Aid to Families with Dependant Children (AFDC) and a few other smaller programs beginning in 1997, received close to $25 billion in 2000. The total spent on this controversial category is less than six percent of the total spent by government for "low-income" persons.

The Statistical Abstract of the United States also provides information about private philanthropy. In 2000, American individuals, foundations, and corporations donated over $228 billion to charitable causes. Table 6.2 shows the contributions:

Table 6.2
Source of Funds Contributed in the US in the Year 2000[5]

Source of Funds	Contributions (in billions)
Individuals	$175.1
Foundations	$24.6
Corporations	$10.7
Charitable bequests	$17.8
TOTAL	**$228.3**

Individuals contributed over 75 percent of the total. Table 6.3 shows the kinds of organizations receiving contributions. Religious organizations received the largest amount.

We see immediately that charitable contributions from all sources (from individuals, corporations, foundations, and bequests) and for all causes (from the American Cancer Society to the Wilderness Society) amounts to less than one-half of the cost of caring for the country's needy. But there is hope in some quarters of persuading Americans to give more. To see whether that is a realistic proposal, we need to have some idea of how much we already donate.

Table 6.3
Destination of Funds Contributed by
Private Philanthropy in the Year 2000[6]

Destination of Funds	Contributions (in billions)
Religion	$77.0
Education	$31.7
Health	$18.8
Human service	$18.0
Arts, culture, humanities	$11.5
Public/societal benefit	$11.6
Environment, wildlife	$6.2
International	$3.7
Gifts to foundations	$24.7
Unallocated	$25.2
TOTAL	**$228.3**

Since contributions to those in need of support have not been a major category reported to the public,[7] we need to try to extract an estimate from available data. Clearly, a portion of contributions from some categories, e.g. Religion and Human Service, is donated to the economically disadvantaged, while it is likely that very little if any would be expected to come from the categories of Environment/Wildlife or Arts, Culture and Humanities.

The process of estimating private contributions to the needy appears in Appendix I. After deriving an upper limit of giving, we can say with some confidence that private contributions to the economically disadvantaged were no more than $45 billion in the year 2000. They might have been substantially less, but we can't be sure. What is clear is that private contributions amounted about 10 percent of what government spent on this population. The magnitude of the difference between the calculated upper limit of private giving and government giving is illustrated in Figure 6.1. For Americans to increase their voluntary giving ten-fold for those in need seems quite unrealistic.

Figure 6.1

Calculated Upper Limit of Private Spending and Public Spending for the Economically Disadvantaged in the 2000

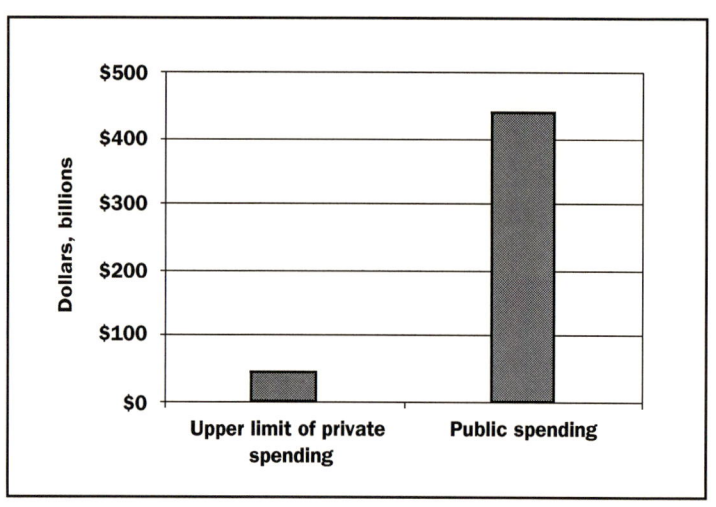

The Right has promoted several changes in tax policy to motivate taxpayers to increase voluntary giving. The Charity, Aid, Recovery and Empowerment Act (CARE), passed by the Senate in April, 2003, permits deductions up to $250 for individual taxpayers ($500 for married couples) who do not itemize. This last-mentioned group is a substantial portion, 65 to 70 percent, of all taxpayers. The net increase in contributions estimated by the Congressional Budget Office (CBO) is 0.5 to 2.9 percent.[8] For those in need, this increase would be barely noticeable.

President George W Bush proposed a more ambitious change in tax policy in 1999: to allow those who don't itemize to deduct 100 percent of charitable contributions up to the standard deduction appropriate for their filing status. In a study by commissioned by Independent Sector,[9] PriceWaterhouseCoopers estimates that additional contributions would amount to $14.6 billion. If the projected additional giving were to follow the pattern of current giving, up to 20 percent would go to the needy. Recalling that total government payments to this population was approximately $437 billion, the additional $2.9 billion (at best) that might be collected by this more extensive tax change still falls substantially short of what is required.

If reasonable changes in tax deductions are not likely to help very much, could additional attention focused on the needy persuade Americans to give more? A few years ago we had a chance to see what Americans contributed when confronted with an overwhelmingly tragic event, September 11. The Better Business Bureau serving Metropolitan New York reports, "For many, the drive to help with relief efforts served deeply personal needs, as well as spiritual and patriotic purposes."[10] As of July 2003 organizations reported contributions of $2.8 billion (including approximately $500 million in grants that were "necessarily" counted twice). The reader can compare that generous outpouring under very special circumstances with what government now provides for the economically disadvantaged.

Therefore, we can restate the question asked at the outset of this chapter. Are you willing to increase your charitable contributions by ten-fold in order to care for those in need in this country? Do you think everyone else will? While some individuals might respond generously, the vast majority of Americans, even with tax incentives, will not contribute an amount remotely adequate to replace government aid to the needy in our society. But the current situation is even worse. There are indications that Americans will be giving even less, and it is not because we are becoming less generous.

A recent challenge to American largesse comes from new causes competing with traditional charitable needs. Consider the following survey results: In 2002 the Association of Fund-Raising Distributors and Suppliers[11] reported that its members sold $1.9 billion of products that were then resold for fundraising purposes. Eighty percent (about $1.5 billion) were sold to schools and school-related groups. Anyone who has or has had children in school knows about such fundraising. To the amount quoted above must be added fundraising from bake sales, car washes, and scrip sales.

Traditionally these school sales raised money to buy sports or band equipment, team uniforms, field trips, and other needed but unessential items. More recently, many such sales fund teachers and other core educational needs. According to *The Chronicle of Philanthropy*,[12] "Many school districts have full-time fund raisers, and are working to attract wealthy individuals—even those who don't have kids in the schools—to give money. And as local governments face serious budget shortfalls, many experts expect that public schools will become even fiercer competitors for philanthropic dollars."

While most public school groups raise under $150,000 a year, much larger funds are being raised around the country, often with the help of foundations. The *Chronicle of Philathropy* gives examples.[13] "The Public Education Foundation, in Chattanooga, Tenn., received a pledge of $6.5-million over five years from two local foundations, the Benwood and the W.H. Osborne Foundations. The charity is now trying to raise $3 million in additional donations needed to match the foundation grants. The money will be used to improve third-grade reading levels and teacher education at nine low-performing elementary schools." Here is another approach: "The Irvine Public Schools Foundation, in California, raised $4.3 million last year, a large portion of which will help ensure that state cuts won't affect the school district's small class size for kindergarten through third grade. The group has set a fund-raising goal of $6 million annually by 2005. Among the group's revenue raisers: a program to refurbish donated musical instruments and then rent them to students. Last year about 1,000 students rented cellos, French horns, trumpets, and other instruments, bringing in $300,000 in income. 'We are really focusing on being a well-run nonprofit business and not thinking of ourselves as a little public-school foundation,' says Tim Shaw, the group's executive director."

This new fundraising for public schools raises important issues. First, it lets government off the hook. As Linda Hodge, president of National Parent Teachers Association (PTA) in Chicago put it, "They don't raise enough money to make a huge difference, but they raise enough money to quiet people down so that it's not that hot an issue." Second is the concern about equity. Schools in poor neighborhoods don't have the professional fundraising staff, parents with wealth, and the free time to volunteer for fundraising, foundations, or corporate supporters to match schools in higher income neighborhoods. "If not done well or thoughtfully, this type of private fund raising has the potential to exacerbate the gaps between rich and poor schools," according to Howard Schaffer, a spokesman for the Public Education Network, a national association of local education foundations.[14]

Private fundraising for the core functions of public schools just described is an example of the type of charity we may see more of if conservatives have their way. As right-wing politicians pressure public budgets to shrink, increasing demands will be placed on private largesse. The needs of those with limited incomes will face competition from causes newly "released" from public treasuries. When those with middle and upper incomes see their own interests threatened, it is likely that they will contribute to those interests first in the way we have seen with parents of school children.

Before leaving the subject of providing for those in need, we should briefly consider a category of assistance that is given to those who are able-bodied and usually earning a normal income. These funds rarely stir up controversy. They go to those who have suffered a catastrophic loss of property resulting from a natural disaster. For this kind of aid we still use the old term for assistance, "relief." This population is often served by a government agency the Federal Emergency Management Agency (FEMA). For disasters great and small we know that one of this nation's premier nonprofits, the American Red Cross, will be there to help. The Red Cross arrives immediately and provides the shelter, food, and other immediate needs of disaster victims. Yet both im-

Figure 6.2
Average Annual Amount Spent on Disasters by the American Red Cross and FEMA 1995-1999

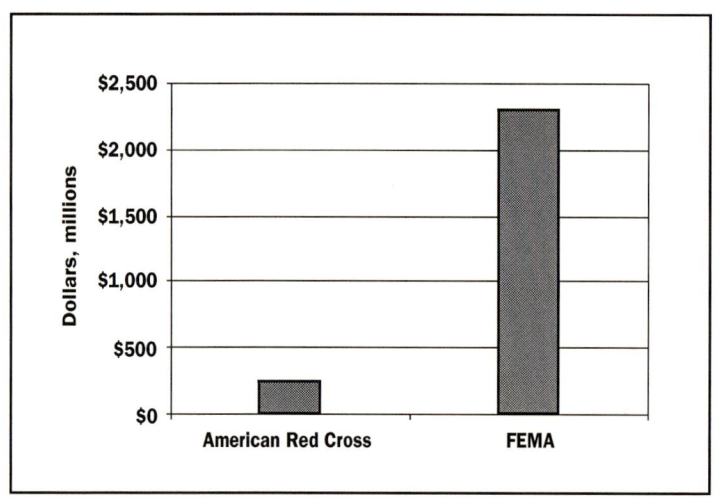

mediate and longer term needs are provided by government, and here too the government outspends the private organization by about ten-to-one. Figure 6.2 illustrates the magnitude of the difference. The average annual amount spent for disaster relief by FEMA during the period of 1995 through 1999 was $2.3 billion per year.[15] During the same period the American Red Cross spent an average of $235.7 million per year for the same purpose.[16]

Disaster relief, unlike aid to the society's needy, seems like a good candidate to hand over to the private sector. Disasters get ample attention in the media, and the amounts needed are close to amounts nonprofits have raised for other reasons. Agencies, such as the Red Cross, are already established. Many who receive disaster relief are property owners and therefore earning a decent salary. Curiously, this rather obvious candidate for privatization has not been taken up by conservatives. It appears that after losing homes to hurricanes, tornadoes, fires or flood, conservatives, like most Americans, are unwilling to depend on the kindness of strangers.

Many conservatives believe in a second front against poverty: faith-based initiatives. These initiatives are not usually directed towards all in need. The elderly poor, the physically disabled, and the mentally disabled are not usually targets of such initiatives even though these groups are, according to religious teaching, worthy recipients of charitable attention. Rather, faith-based initiatives typically address those whose poverty may be related to drug addiction, crime, violence, and broken families. In other words these programs address problems conservatives believe can be resolved by a change of heart, the inspiration of faith. Conservatives believe in developing personal relationships with those whom they help. In some but not all cases they also promote developing personal relationships with their Savior.

Faith-based initiatives have successfully assaulted some inner-city problems commonly believed to be beyond hope or with poor odds for improvement. The controversies which faith-based initiatives have stimulated around separation of church and state and hiring by these groups have been much discussed. Here we consider several questions that have received little attention.

Teen Challenge is one of the most successful faith based organizations. Addicts who successfully complete this program have been able to replace addiction with religion. A high percentage of those who complete the year-long residential program succeed in remaining drug free. Most drug treatment programs are not able to treat those with addiction for a full year. It's highly unlikely that an insurance company or the state would pay for treatment of that length of time. Is length of treatment related to outcome? A large-scale government study which followed those who spent varying amounts of time in treatment found that "controlling for type of treatment (and therefore planned length of stay), length of stay is associated with the extent of decrease in drug use."[17] Also, it would be irrational for an organization that invests so much in each individual to be careless about whom it admits. Teen Challenge must choose those who are strongly motivated to lead a drug-free life. The curriculum is deeply religious. Drop-outs have complained of "Too much religion."[18] The question of an applicant's readiness or motivation is important in this as in other faith-based initiatives. We would expect those who voluntarily enter a treatment program to be more motivated than those who are required by a court order or an employer.

Another faith-based organization that gains participants voluntarily is the Prison Fellowship Ministries (PFM).[19] Started by Chuck Colson of Watergate fame, PFM uses many volunteers and paid staff to provide education, drug-treatment, and religious instruction to prisoners during and after incarceration. It also has programs for their families, including mentoring at-risk youth and purchase and delivery of gifts to children of prisoners at Christmas. A brief summary of the results for one of their programs behind bars provides a perspective on this organization's work and success.[20] In April 1997, PFM began a collaboration with the Texas Department of Criminal Justice. Staffed mainly with volunteers, the comprehensive program—"expressly Christian in orientation"—included "education, work, life skills, values restructuring, and one-on-one mentoring in an environment where religious instruction permeates all aspects of the prison environment." Participants had to remain in the program 16 to 24 months while in prison and for 6 to 12 months in an after-care program after release. In order to complete the after care program, participants had to hold a job and be an active member of a church at least three of the first six months following release.

To create a study pool and to track results, participants had to have the potential of being out of prison for at least two years by September, 2002.

PFM found 177 participants who met the requirements of the study's time frame as well as those of the prison. Of these, 75 completed the program, 51 were paroled early, 24 voluntarily quit, 19 were removed for disciplinary reasons, and 1 was removed for medical reasons. The recidivism and re-arrest rates of the 75 who completed the program were compared to a matched group of 1,754 inmates who met the program's criteria but who did not participate. During the two years after release, 17 percent of program graduates and 35 percent of the matched group were arrested. In the same period 8 percent of the graduates and 20 percent of the matched group were incarcerated. Among all participants, including those who did and did not complete the program, 36 percent were arrested compared with 35 percent of the matched group, and 24% were incarcerated compared to 20 percent of the matched group. Mentoring was associated with lower rates of recidivism.

The sustained attention of a volunteer would be expected to make a difference in the life of a prisoner or the child of a prisoner (or any child with one absent parent or with some other special need). To what degree programs such as PFM are successful because of such attention is difficult to say. To their credit, PFM's volunteers (and trained staff) are present and paying sustained attention, when most of society ignores this population.

To illustrate the effect of personal attention even in the absence of a religious environment, we can look at the results of a study of Big Brothers Big Sisters (BBBS). It is a secular organization that has been doing good works for about one hundred years. Its "primary mission is of one-to-one mentoring with friendship as its cornerstone."[21] It does require a sustained commitment from its volunteers. A volunteer can spend as little as an hour once a week, but must do it much more than once.

In a study of BBBS's mentoring of a group of youngsters many of whom were low-income members of minorities, many benefits were found. In the group studied, volunteers mentored an average of three to four hours three times a month for at least a year.[22] BBBS follows a "set of operational guidelines about screening, matching, training, supervising and monitoring." When interviewed 18 months after their mentoring experience Little Brothers and Little Sisters were found to be 46 percent less likely to initiate drug use during the study period than those who remained on waiting lists (the control group), 27 percent less likely to start alcohol use, and 33 percent less likely to hit someone. Little Brothers and Little Sisters skipped half as many days of school as the control youth and had "modest" improvements in their school grades. Several of the effects mentioned here, as well as others described in the study, were more pronounced among minority youth.

Professor John J. Dilulio, Jr of the University of Pennsylvania, who more than anyone else has given faith-based initiatives intellectual respectability, says about the study of Big Brothers Big Sisters, "Evaluation called attention to at least two problems. First, thousands of eligible children remained on waiting lists due to a shortage of available mentors. Second, the inner-city youths who most needed responsible non-parental adult support and guidance in their lives were the least likely to get it. The simple reason is that Big Brothers Big Sisters of America... attracts youths who already have at least one parent, guardian or other adult in their lives who is responsible enough to sign them up, follow through on interviews and phone calls, fill out forms and so forth." In a follow-up study, Public/Private Ventures found that "as many as a quarter of youth in 'moderately poor' neighborhoods were completely 'disconnected' from 'positive adult supports.'"[23]

Where will the Big Brothers and Big Sister volunteers be found to help the thousands of children on waiting lists? A number of attempts at recruiting through churches have been made. When mentors are found, young people benefit, but waiting lists endure. A study of attempts to use churches to recruit mentors for high-risk youths in four cities found that "The two main challenges arise in recruiting a sufficient number of mentors and maintaining the matches over time, which requires intensive case management." The study went on to say, "The difficulty finding male and younger mentors who may be more attuned to youth culture might simply reflect the demographics of many African American congregations, and is therefore likely to be a challenge for any faith-based organization operating a mentoring program for similar youth."[24]

Personal contact over a period of time certainly seems to be a factor in the success of faith based initiatives, but it is not the whole story. Religious commitment and involvement benefit inner-city youths. In a review of studies of the effect of religion on health and social welfare Byron Johnson found 46 studies on delinquency. In 78 percent religion was associated with lower delinquency. He concludes, "There is mounting evidence that religious involvement may lower the risks of a broad range of delinquent behaviors, including both minor and serious forms of criminal behavior."[25] In 54 studies of religion and drug use, 87 percent were better off with religious participation, and in 97 studies of religion and alcohol abuse, 94 percent were better of with religion in their lives. [26]

In addition to providing a positive influence on young people, religious institutions help those in need in other ways. Organizations like Catholic Charities and Lutheran Social Services provide significant assistance to the poor. Houses of worship are also a source of help. Mark Chaves and William Tsitsos studied a nationally representative sample of 1,236 U.S. religious congregations.[27] They found that 57 percent of the congregations provided some sort of help to those with limited incomes, usually emergency needs of food, clothing, and shelter. "Other activities, especially activities requiring more sustained, face-to-face contact with the needy, are more rare." Only 6 percent of the congregations had someone on staff dedicated at least 25 percent of the time to social service projects. Contrary to the expectations of many in the faith-based community, most U.S. congregations provide only "fleeting contact" with the recipients of their aid and not the holistic, personal, or transformational contact that is needed to change lives. However, Chaves and Tsitsos also found that a majority (84 percent) of congregations collaborated with others providing social services, usually another congregation or secular agency, and some of their "evidence points to the possibility that collaborations with government and with secular organizations might encourage exactly the kind of social service activities some claim to be the distinctive preserve of religious organizations."[28]

The work of Chaves and Tsitsos has been compared to that of Ram Cnaan, whose work is often cited by those in the faith-based community. Cnaan and Boddie studied[29] a sample of congregations (with smaller ones under-represented) and included many more activities in his list of social services than Chaves and Tsitsos did. In addition to clothing closets, food pantries, and scholarships, which would be targeted to those with limited incomes, his list of social services included international relief (which would, of course, not help local people), music performances, supporting and participating in interfaith coalitions, non-religious holiday celebrations, summer day camps, hospital visitation, recreational programs for the elderly, and others. Not surprisingly, he found a higher percent of congregations involved in social services that did Chaves and Tsitsos. Yet in the work of Cnaan and Boddie, it is difficult to extract that portion of social services that would help the needy (see also Appendix I).

The sample of faith–based projects and studies just described shows there to be good evidence that faith can be a factor in ameliorating the lives of those in need. But if it's clear that faith is a factor, it is also clear that it is just that, a factor, and not the total answer to the problems of the urban ghetto. There has been no institution more ubiquitous in the inner city than the church. The problems in low-income urban communities have eluded not only the government and the non-profit sector; they have also eluded the church. As those to the left of center must acknowledge the positive effects of faith, those to the right of center need to recognize the need for contributions from the government and the secular community. They also need to understand that to claim that those who dedicate their lives to the underprivileged have nothing to offer unless imbued with religious spirit is profoundly insulting and unfair to millions of dedicated social activists, social workers and volunteers. Cnaan and Boddie said of American congregations that they are "neither a panacea for all of society's problems nor a substitute for public sector support."[30] The same must be said of private charity and faith-based initiatives.

CHAPTER SEVEN

How One State Has Fared

In this chapter I turn from the national scene to describe the effects of two years of political domination by no-tax-increase conservatives in one state, the one where I have lived all my life. Warning: there is little good news to report.

Minnesota has been known as a land of lakes and liberals. The state's most famous political son, Hubert Humphrey, was the quintessential liberal. Walter Mondale, Orville Freeman and Eugene McCarthy were his colleagues. Paul Wellstone was his political descendent. Minnesota's Republicans called themselves "Independent," and shared a strong commitment to education and health care with those on the other side of the aisle. The political atmosphere was clean and civil.

The state has historically had high taxes, but also high services, standards of living, and quality of life. Education at all levels was strongly supported. Philanthropy has been very active. For most in the state life has been good.

Minnesota business people used to routinely complain that the state's high taxes would drive some of their number away. In 1991 the legislature directed a study of businesses leaving Minnesota. For nearly ten years the Department of Trade and Economic Development surveyed manufacturing companies that stopped operating in the state. They questioned 1,606 firms and verified that one hundred (6%, range per year was five to sixteen) left.[1] Some, but not all, complained of property taxes. Complaints have been less common in recent years.

To those who live in other parts of the country, Minnesota has often been considered part of fly-over land. It may come as a surprise to read that this state or its major metropolitan area (the Twin Cities of St. Paul and Minneapolis,) has found itself on many top-ten lists. Here are a few:

- Second in Morgan Quitno's Livable State ranking after being number one since 1996.[2] The award is based on 42 factors.
- Fifth in Morgan Quitno's Healthiest State[3] The ranking is based upon 21 factors.
- Eighth in the Milkin National State Technology and Science Index, 2004[4]
- Fourth in the rate of volunteering[5]
- Minneapolis is seventh in The New Creativity Index[6]
- The state was third in the United Way State of Caring Index in amount raised by United Way per capita, based on 2001 data[7]
- Minneapolis-St Paul are fifth in the World Knowledge Competitiveness Index in 2003, first in 2002[8]

Yet not everything is rosy. University of Minnesota faculty salaries are twenty-eighth on a list of thirty of the top private and public research institutions.[9] Problems such as rural and urban poverty and racial achievement gaps in urban schools persist.

In the last decade or so liberalism has lost the allegiance of many Minnesotans. To paraphrase favorite son, Bob Dylan, the times they've been a'changing. Half of Minnesota's delegation in the House of Representatives is now Democrat, half Republican. In the 1990s state public spending grew more slowly in Minnesota than elsewhere in the nation. The state ranked eighteenth in the nation in number of workers (state and local) per capita. Recently, we have been led by two decidedly non-liberal minority governors.

Third parties have played an important role in the election of these minority governors. The first, a former wrestler, might have been called a libertarian with a different persona. He called himself an independent and won the governorship with 37 percent of the vote to 34 percent for the Republican candidate and 28 percent for the Democratic candidate. A fiscal conservative and a social liberal, he "refunded" the state's surplus to the citizens, and pressed for lower taxes and public spending. A favorite anecdote was his description of a worker who earned $100 a day digging holes and then had to give up $35 to people who did nothing to help dig the hole. A Democratic legislative leader eventually pointed out that a worker earning that wage would pay a maximum of $16 in federal, state and local taxes. Another famous adage of this one-term governor was that if you're smart enough to go to college, you're smart enough to figure out how to pay for it.

Pressure on the public sector to make do with less had been exerted for many years when Minnesotans went to the polls in 2002. Voters again faced three major candidates for governor at the polling place. This time a conservative Republican won 44 percent of the vote to 36 percent for the Democrat, 16 percent for the Independent, and 2% for the Green candidate. Walter Mondale, a late stand-in for the recently deceased incumbent Paul Wellstone, lost the Senatorial election with 47 percent of the vote to Republican Norm Coleman's 50 percent (Jim Moore, the Independent, received 2 percent).

Conservatives in the state have been ably assisted by the Taxpayers League of Minnesota. This organization has persuaded many elected officials to sign a "No New Taxes" pledge. According to its website[10] those who sign the Taxpayer Protection Pledge promise to "oppose (and vote against/veto) any and all efforts to increase taxes." It is more strongly worded than the analogous national pledge (about which more in the next chapter). The pledge has been signed by the new U.S. Senator (who also signed the national pledge), four U.S. Congressmen, and the Governor, Lieutenant Governor, Secretary of State, State Auditor and the Speaker of the Minnesota House of Representatives elected in 2002. In addition 18 out of 67 state senators and 40 of 134 state representatives have signed it.

One of Taxpayers League's most interesting press releases was issued on the fifth day of a Metro Transit strike in March of 2004. The League, strongly opposed to public support of bus transportation, made a suggestion that, it said, "might save taxpayers billions of dollars—and really help people in poverty who genuinely are transit dependent: let's buy them used cars. 10,000 used cars at $5000 would cost only $50 million—a fraction of what we spend each year to run the bus system. We could buy 40,000 good used cars for lower income people and still have money left over—from just one year's worth of transit operating costs."[11] The League did not suggest a solution for two other groups who routinely use buses, the elderly and students.

As the State Legislature convened early in 2002, Minnesota, like many others states, was suffering from a recession-induced budget deficit—in Minnesota's case: $4.3 billion. The Governor had a majority in the legislature's House of Representatives, but not in the Senate.

Four former Minnesota governors, three Republicans and one Democrat, criticized the newly elected governor for his no-new-taxes pledge. They expressed concern that the disadvantaged would suffer the most from budget cuts. They advocated a balanced approach of spending cuts and tax increases. Each had faced budget problems after election, and each solved those problems with a variety of tax increases. One of the Republicans said, "You cannot deny the right to basic health care.... It is wrong. The pain should be spread, and that means a tax increase—particularly on those of us who can afford it."[12] The new governor, a congenial politician with an engaging smile, said, without apology, that those who use government the most must expect to take the biggest hit.[13]

Minnesota citizens knew a new kind of elected official was in office when the recently elected state auditor claimed that "local government aid" (funds allocated by the state to local government) could be cut in half without damaging essential services, which she defined as police, fire, maintenance, and basic administration. She asserted that state aid should not be provided to cities for non-essential services such as parks, youth recreation, libraries, airports, transit and homeless shelters.[14]

The legislature adjourned at the end of May 2003 after a "contentious and hard-fought" session. The legislators addressed the $4.3 billion deficit with spending cuts mainly to local communities and health and human services, accounting shifts, and "one time resources." The conservative agenda became evident in non-budget legislation: It became much easier to carry a concealed weapon, and a woman seeking an abortion would have to receive specific information and wait at least 24 hours before having the procedure.[15] In the absence of tax increases at the state level, citizens widely anticipated property tax boosts, although the state limits the amount of taxes that local government can raise. Metropolitan area property tax increases were double-digit, but in many outlying areas they were in single digits. A growing number of cities raised utility franchise fees which will be passed on to home and business property owners.[16]

It didn't take long for effects of spending cuts to be felt. Here are some of effects on health care changes to predominantly low-income residents:

> ▸ An estimated 38,000 Minnesotans stood to lose state-subsidized health insurance at a time when Minnesotans, who were losing their jobs and therefore their health insurance, were looking to the government for assistance.[17]

- Medical aid which pays for supplemental insurance to about 4,000 families with disabled children for items such as wheelchairs and personal aides is to be based on a family's adjusted gross income. Families could see their monthly fees go up as much a four-fold. While some will easily afford the increases, those who cannot may be forced to institutionalize their children. This program was set up to keep the disabled at home.[18]
- As part of the cuts to a state-subsidized health insurance program called Minnesota Care, coverage for medical supplies for adults without children was eliminated. As a result diabetics can no longer buy glucose test strips with a $3 co-pay. They will have to pay nearly $100 a month for the strips.[19] Low-income asthmatics and diabetics are at risk for "catastrophic incidents."[20]
- In 2004, because the state share of the AIDS Drug Assistance Program for low income AIDS patients fell by 1 percent while the number of eligible patients grew by 50 percent (since 2001), state officials are raising the amount recipients pay for their premiums and for their co-pays. In addition, state officials are considering a waiting list. Eleven states already have waiting lists, and ten have reduced benefits. Advocates for AIDS patients point out that the state's actions increase the risk that poor patients will abandon treatment. If that happens, control of the spread of AIDS will be compromised.[21]
- Among the effects on the elderly are new higher charges for home-delivered meals, housekeeping assistance, and nursing visits. If the frail elderly can not afford new fees, the state is now entitled to put a lien on their homes. The memorandum of a fiscal analyst for the Senate revealed that the intended effect was to scare seniors away from the program altogether. In that way—not by collecting higher fees or liens—the state could expect to save $9 million. The memo also predicted that one in four

who might have used home care would instead wind up in a nursing home.[22]
- Low-income residents qualifying for medical assistance must pay $1 for each generic drug prescription and $3 for each brand name drug prescription up to $20 per month. Clinic and physician services for non-preventive visits are to cost $3 per appointment. Dental coverage is limited to $500 per year except for emergency treatment, extraction for dentures and dentures. Children under 21 years of age, pregnant women and several other groups are exempt from the above co-pays and restrictions.[23]
- UCare of Minnesota, the HMO serving those on government funded health care programs, is having difficulty finding dentists to serve low-income patients because of the new annual cap ($500) on dental services.[24]

Low-income residents charged with a crime were required to pay for public defense services according to the seriousness of the charge: $50 for a misdemeanor, $100 for a gross misdemeanor, and $200 for a felony. No waiver was allowed. A few months after the law went into effect, a Hennepin County judge declared it unconstitutional. Previously, a $28 co-pay was required for all services, and a judge was allowed to waive the fee for clients unable to pay.[25]

Not all Legislative cuts affected low income people. Effects, great and small, were felt by most Minnesotans. A sampling:

- Minneapolis Park Board funds were inadequate to maintain and repair seven fountains in the city. Private funds were found to keep all but one operating. However, needed repairs are on hold.[26]
- The Minnesota Zoo receives 39 percent of its operating revenues from taxpayers, compared to 50 percent for zoos nationwide.

Staffing at the end of 2003 was lower than it had been at the Zoo's opening in 1978. Continuing budget cuts have made admission price increases necessary, and attendance has been dropping five years in a row.[27]

- Minneapolis Public Libraries cut 75 staff positions (bringing the total to 262), reduced hours or reclassified down another 62 positions, and reduced hours at all libraries. The Central Library is now open a total of 40 hours a week over six days. On three days of the week it is open five hours, and on the remainder seven hours. Branch library hours vary from twenty to forty hours. Branches are open three to five days. In addition to books and other media, libraries provide computers to those who do not have them at home. Parents of students with projects requiring library work have found the changes maddening.[28]

- Reduced hours and staffing cuts were common in many cities and counties. Anoka County, birthplace of Garrison Keillor, reduced library hours, park hours and service desk hours, and discontinued lifeguards at county beaches. The county will have fewer probation services for juveniles, fewer summer youth jobs and fewer truancy programs. A teen pregnancy prevention program is being discontinued.[29]

- The mayor of tiny Belgrade (population 750), tried to drop charges against a drunken driver, because a court case would have eaten up the city's entire criminal prosecution budget. The city had lost nearly $50,000 in state aid. He was overruled by his City Council.[30]

Non-profits suffered but adapted to the increased needs and decreased funds brought on by the recession, and some suffered legislative cuts. The new governor had suggested in his campaign that Minnesota's nonprofits and foundations take on a bigger role in caring for those in need.

- Second Harvest Heartland, a major hunger relief organization, restructured in order to become more efficient by reducing staff from 90 to 73 and by renovating its warehouse to the tune of $1.8 million. Rack storage space was tripled, and computerized barcodes now enable more rapid movement of foodstuffs to 850 non-profit agencies who serve the needy. The organization faces decreasing donations from food companies who are watching inventories more carefully and are sometimes selling excess to secondary markets. The organization now uses only 4 percent of its budget for administration and fundraising.[31]
- Twin Cities Habitat for Humanity announced cuts of 12 from its staff of 77 and reduced 2 more positions in 2004. The organization has recently been unable to build as many houses as it projected. The reasons are several: a shortage of vacant lots, increased construction costs, and longer time-frames for each project. In the last five years, the cost of building a home, including materials and hiring subcontractors has gone from $60,000 to $72,000. During the same period the cost of buying land and preparing a site for construction has risen from $9,000 to $40,000.[32] "Twin Cities Habitat has built or rehab-ed more than 500 homes since 1985."[33] On the same day the St. Paul Public Housing Agency presented its proposed solution to a $3 million reduction in Federal Section 8 funds. HUD has reduced funds for this rent assistance program that helps about 4,000 low-income St. Paulites make up the difference between 30 percent of their income and the amount they pay in rent. The program has a waiting list of 4,400 families.[34] (The city and state make no contribution to this program.)

- State payment was eliminated for a mentoring program serving 25 youths with mental-health problems. Save Our Sons offers this program to primarily black youth, and also receives funding for them from other sources. The mother of a youngster with serious anger problems described how the agency was available day or night to counsel or intervene if problems at home became too much to bear.[35]
- Minnesota Project Innovation, a non-profit that helps small Minnesota businesses get federal contracts through several federal grants and procurement programs lost its $1.5 million grant from the pro-business governor's budget.[36]
- By the end of 2004 Minnesota State Patrol will stop transporting eyes—which they have often done by relay—from hospitals and funeral homes to the Lions Eye Bank at the University of Minnesota. Since staffing has not kept up with increased traffic on state highways, troopers are overburdened and will have to curtail 42 years of vision-saving volunteering. The Eye Bank, itself a non-profit, has contributed over 14,000 corneal transplants since 1960.[37]
- In 2003 Catholic Charities cut 15 percent of its workforce, 88 workers, and closed two programs. One served young children, and the other provided transitional housing to teenagers with problems who were either referred by the courts or who had just been released from institutions. Other arrangements were made for those served in both programs. Catholic Charities, like others of its ilk, is supported by contributions (including the Annual Catholic Appeal), government, and other funds such as the United Way.[38]

As part of its budget-cutting actions, the Hennepin County Board of Commissioners voted to cut the chaplaincy staff in correctional facilities by two-thirds, which would leave only two part time chaplains to cover three prisons and 8,000 inmate counseling sessions a year, train volunteers, and recruit 350 pastor visits. The Commissioners are aware of the reduced recidivism associated with faith activities. Private donations and Board reconsideration restored part of the funding.[39] Pressure to cut chaplain staffing has been going on for many years. State and county officials think that volunteers should be found for these positions. Volunteers, when they can be found, not only lack the training of chaplains, they also are not able to deal with the ecumenical demands that these positions require.

Some months after attempts to cut chaplain staffing, Minnesota's first significant faith based grant was awarded to Greater Minneapolis Council of Churches. They will disperse over $500,000 to 41 organizations. An additional $530,000 is expected in the fall of 2004, and plans for $700,000 in 2005 are in the works.[40]

Subsidies for child care were reduced. Ramsey County, which includes the state capital of St. Paul, found that 212 families terminated child-care aid during the summer of 2003. Over one-third of these have had to cut back on work hours or quit their jobs, and nearly one-fifth are planning to apply for public assistance.[41] Results were similar in Hennepin County which includes the city of Minneapolis. Welfare workers have noticed that some working parents are taking their names off a waiting list for childcare subsidies. They assume they will never reach the top of the long waiting list, or if they do, will find the new higher co-pays unaffordable. An estimate of welfare costs to the state for these families might be $1,000 per month, instead of the $200 subsidy they would have received for child care before the program was changed to save costs.[42]

The most widely felt losses in the state were in the area of education—from pre-kindergarten to the states colleges and universities. Although the governor promised to hold education harmless when cuts in were made in the 2003 legislative session, the final bill cut $180 million from public schools, "including $70 million for special education, $25 million for summer school and after school programs, and $46 million for compensatory aid to disadvantaged children and $3 million for Head Start." Statewide, 2,000 teachers were laid off.[43]

- ▶ In its fourth year of budget cutting, Minneapolis Public Schools is reducing staff by 700 (including 307 teachers and 98 classroom aides). It is also cutting 175 classrooms. Both declining enrollment and reduced state aid made the reductions necessary.[44] Average class size will rise to 36 students in the 2004-2005 academic year; in 1990 it was 26.[45]
- ▶ Twin Cities suburbs, faced with both declining enrollment and budget crunches, are closing schools. For example, Bloomington, home to Mall of America, had 25,000 students in 24 schools a few decades ago. Now it has 10,500 students in 15 schools. Kindergarten enrollment has declined four years in a row. Formerly, the influx of young families maintained school populations. Now older couples are remaining in their homes longer than they used to, because they are healthy longer and because affordable housing remains hard to find. And more single people are buying homes.[46]
- ▶ At middle class Anoka High School, students have to pay $310 to play hockey and $120 to participate in theater. Teacher vacancies may not be filled in spite of voter approval of a $25 million tax increase for schools. The newly authorized funds are a temporary way to "avert the impact" of state cuts.[47]
- ▶ Parents in one prosperous Twin Cities suburb have raised $800,000 since forming an alliance in 2000 to "preserve and enhance education." It has given over $470,000 to save about twelve teaching positions, improve music and athletic programs, bring back foreign language classes and purchase supplies. The school

district still faced almost a million dollar shortfall in spite of a tax increase approved the previous fall. Another suburb's schools, over half of whose students receive-reduced price lunches, mobilized parents to volunteer at schools in mainly administrative tasks. A third suburb raised $60,000 a few years earlier to retain two science teachers slated for elimination. In the last-mentioned case, the school board eventually prohibited such fundraising.[48]

➤ Minnesota's State Colleges and the University's Board of Trustees passed a tuition increase averaging 12.5% for the state's colleges and universities for 2003-2004 and another increase of the same size for 2004-2005. These increases make it four years in a row that students face double-digit increases in tuition. The increases, along with cost cutting, are needed to make up for the deficit of $191.5 million caused by reduced allocations agreed to by the governor and the legislature.[49]

An acting Superintendent of Minneapolis Schools, a Republican and former speaker of the Minnesota House of Representatives said, "The public, by and large, supports public education, but a number of the policymakers do not. I'm not a conspiracy theorist. I've never been to Roswell, New Mexico (where those aliens crash-landed, in UFO mythology). But the politicians who are beating up on us say we're failing. And, by their actions, they can set the system up to fail. Some of their decisions have done just that. That's what they have in mind."[50]

The 2004 Legislative session had less budget work to do but did consider a major bonding bill at a time of very low interest rates. But the session ended in gridlock. Compromise could not be reached on the bonding bill or any other major legislation. The Governor did not actively promote compromise toward the end of the session, and didn't seem to feel any responsibility for the outcome. Here as in Washington the buck no longer stops at the top. Among the few bills to pass was one allowing a hunting season for mourning doves. The state Senate, dominated by Democrats, does not face election in the fall of 2004; the state House of Representatives, dominated by Republicans, faces the voters in November 2004.

One of the reasons for the legislative gridlock is the presence of a new kind right wing Republican who, like the President, listens to a Higher Advisor. For example the Minnesota Secretary of State told attendees at a National Day of Prayer breakfast that "separation of church and state was a destructive idea." A suburban legislator wrote to a constituent that "It is legal for a state to establish and promote a religion." When questioned later, he said he didn't plan to do so. Finally, a state senator, who has been vigorously promoting a constitutional amendment to ban same-sex marriages, took a group of supporters into an empty Senate chamber to pray around the desks of senators, including those who oppose her proposed amendment.[51] What we did not hear from these religious, elected representatives were any reports of concern for those hurt by state budget cuts.

To Democrats and many Republicans, Minnesota has taken a wrong right turn. One of those Republicans, Minnesota's oldest living governor, 95 year old Elmer L. Anderson, has just published his second book, *I Trust to Be Believed,* a collection of his speeches and reflections on a life which so far has included 75 years as a business executive, state senator, governor and community leader. Interviewed on the occasion of the book's debut he spoke of Minnesota's plight. "We're off the track and out of gear." He summarized a long-held view of the state, "We were a high-tax state when I was governor, and we still are, but since that time we went from below-average income to above-average income and from an out-migration state to an in-migration state. The facts don't support the contention that the best government is the cheapest government."[52]

Whether the new breed of elected representative will prevail remains to be seen. The changes the state has sustained, though unprecedented, are spotty, and busy, hard-working Minnesotans (the state is number one in the nation in that category[53]) may adapt and take them in stride. No known deaths have resulted from the budget cuts so far, and the change in direction may need to pick up more steam before its effects sink in. It is hard to see how this new direction will bring any more distinction to the state. The opposite seems more likely.

CHAPTER EIGHT

Comments, Concerns, and Conclusions

In 1999 candidate George W Bush proposed reducing taxes because the federal government enjoyed a budget surplus during the presidential campaign. After his election President George W. Bush recommended reducing taxes to help the economy out of the developing recession. Once the recession ended President George W. Bush recommended making temporary tax reductions permanent to keep the economy growing. No matter what the economic circumstances, George W. Bush recommends tax cuts. The president seems to believe that the powerful economic engine of the U.S. economy is so frail that it needs constant fiscal stimulus *and* very low interest rates *and* the infusion of billions of dollars from the massive refinancing of mortgages in recent years. In fact, George W. Bush not only favors tax cuts for every occasion, he also opposes tax increases under any and all circumstances.

Though he doesn't say so, the president pledged in writing years ago not to raise taxes. The "Taxpayer Protection Pledge" was the brainchild of Americans for Tax Reform (ATR) led by Grover Norquist. George W. Bush, along with 217 members of the House of Representatives and 42 members of the Senate, have signed the Pledge, which says they will "One, oppose any and all efforts to increase the marginal income tax rates for individuals and/or businesses; and Two, oppose any net reduction or elimination of deductions and credits, unless matched dollar for dollar by further reducing tax rates."[1] Insisting on no tax increases forever assumes a static world where we face no new challenges and continue to face all the traditional ones. So as we take on a war of indefinite duration against terrorism, we are not asked to pay for the new massive spending this war is requires. Even as young Americans daily give their lives and limbs in a distant war, the rest of us are asked to contribute absolutely nothing. It is unseemly. The policies of President George W. Bush and the ATR have a purpose which has nothing to do with the economy. We will come to that shortly.

Whatever G.W. Bush's motives, his claim, shared by the Right, is that our taxes are so high that they cause private investment to shrink and the incentive to work to shrivel. If their view were correct, then our tax burden, which according to the Tax Foundation increased throughout the twentieth century, should have battered our economy into oblivion. But that did not happen.

As described in chapter 2, during the twentieth century the American economy not only grew, but also grew in unprecedented fashion to make us the wealthiest nation in the history of the world. Our longest peacetime economic expansion—and one that created some of the lowest unemployment rates in memory—occurred when our tax burden was the highest of the century. Conservatives may speculate that the economy might have grown even more had we had lower tax rates. But, in the expansion of the 1990s when tax burden was highest, venture capital was plentiful. There was enough to both invest and pay taxes. The shortage that occurred was in employees highly trained in the new areas of information technology. That suggests that we might have been better off had we invested more in the public sector—in education. Speculation, however, is less compelling than facts, and the facts about tax burden during the twentieth century do not support the conservative position.

Other wealthy nations also have relatively high tax burdens. Indeed, each country in a recent "standard of living top ten" had tax burdens greater than our own. The additional tax burdens probably arise because these countries each have comprehensive national health insurance. These countries' high tax burdens did not prevent the Heritage Foundation, a conservative think tank, from ranking four of them (Luxembourg, Ireland, Denmark and Switzerland) in the top ten list of their Index of Economic Freedom. Generally speaking, wealthy countries have high tax burdens, and poor countries have low tax burdens. Four of the ten countries with the highest annual growth in GDP per capita for the period 1995-2000 had tax burdens higher than ours, and one, the "Celtic Tiger," had a burden about just a little larger than ours. Of the ten fastest growing national economies during between 1995 and 2000, only four had tax burdens substantially lower than ours. Finally chapter 3 demonstrates that in modern economies, standard of living bears no relationship to the growth of standard of living. To put it another way, the evidence declares that growing faster will not necessarily increase our standard of living.

If you believe that the economic data I present is simplistic, then I plead guilty, sort of. My argument responds to the Right's equally simplistic economic assertions. The "Tax Protection Pledge" does not speak of any particular kind of taxes; it rejects *all* tax increases. The data I offer in chapters 2 and 3 offers an honest, rigorous look at the economies of the United States and other nations. Claims that taxes have stifled our economic growth contradict the facts. Although "excessive" tax rates, those far higher than we endure, can stifle economies, low taxes also hinder economic growth. Inadequate investment in roads, highways, bridges, education, law enforcement, etc. creates a poor environment for economic growth. The way a government imposes taxes is as important as the tax burden itself. For example the Tax Reform Act of 1986, built upon ideas that Senator Bill Bradley (D, N.J.) introduced in 1982, received presidential and bipartisan support because it applied equitably to eliminate tax loopholes and reduce tax rates.

By contrast, recent conservative claims to reform taxes by eliminating double taxation on dividends is just partisan rhetoric. Income taxes and sales taxes impose double taxation as well, right? Anyone ready to reform that problem? Paying taxes is an onerous duty of citizens who can afford to do so, and that is why demagoguery is a continuing temptation. Those who oppose taxes in principle need to find an unoccupied oil-rich country in which to live. Those who oppose taxation because they believe it hurts the economy need to produce facts. My facts support the opposing position.

President G. W. Bush favors tax cuts in all circumstances, but he has not told us he opposes tax increases in all circumstances. That lack of full disclosure may be related to another, unexpressed goal: to limit future spending. President Reagan recognized that government debt into the foreseeable future restrains future spending. In many ways this policy is the enduring Reagan legacy. If Democrats propose ambitious government programs, then they will have to raise taxes. Conservatives believe that prospect is too onerous for the public to endure. So the Republican administration expands government without raising taxes to fight a war, but because of the resulting budget deficit, they think Democrats will be unable to expand government for any of their programs without raising taxes. Why is it OK for Republicans to create debt but not for Democrats? Why should only the Democrats pay as they go, while Republicans ask future generations to pay for the billions of dollars they spend? It's all red ink. The parties may differ only in how they spill it.

The goal of restraining future spending is part of the conservative goal of reducing the size of government. The Bush administration's attempt to make government more efficient has been very modest in comparison to the programs implemented by the Clinton administration.

But efficiency is not the real conservative goal. The real goal is to reduce the function of government. For conservatives, government costs too much because it does too much. President Reagan expressed the conservative view when he said, "government does nothing as well or as economically as the private sector." Grover Norquist, head of ATR and originator of the "Taxpayer Protection Pledge," told Bill Moyers, "We've set as a conservative movement a goal of reducing the size and cost of [federal and state] government in half in 25 years, which is taking it from a third of the economy down to about 17 percent. . . ."[2]

In response to those who want to shrink government, I argue that our investment in the public sector over the twentieth century increased our freedoms in several ways. We have more freedom of choice in everything from what we do to earn a living to what we do when we retire. These freedoms follow from our economic growth and our investment in public projects such as education and infrastructure. We also have increased our freedom from dishonest and dangerous products by extending the concept of consumer protection against conditions we can not assess. In the same way that buyers for many centuries did not have to bring their own weights to make a purchase of food, we do not have to bring laboratory tests to assess whether the food we buy is free of contamination, or do a personal investigation of a company before we buy its common stock, or be concerned that toys we buy are free from toxic compounds.

Other investments in the public sector expanded or created economic opportunities. For example, investments in basic research expanded the frontiers of knowledge—a value in itself—which provided many opportunities for entrepreneurs to exploit. Consider the Internet.

Our tax dollars have also bought us freedom from many diseases and unhealthy conditions. The private sector certainly contributed to the control and eradication of disease by developing pharmaceuticals and medical devices, but publicly funded research determines the causes of disease and contributes to our understanding of how to manage or eliminate it. We also have relied and must continue to rely on the government to be the arbiter of what is and what is not safe for us to use in treating disease. And a role for government in clean air and clean water is unavoidable, if only because the air and water pollution do not obey borders.

The vast majority of us approve of Social Security and Medicare, although much discussion and more than a little fear mongering have undermined the long-term trust we place in these programs.

Our tax dollars also support projects which are not absolutely necessary and can not be said to increase our freedom. Many are, nevertheless, widely popular: our extra-planetary exploits and the preservation and maintenance of our national parks.

Public money spent preventing problems can pay big rewards. Investment in early childhood programs like Head Start can provide a return better than most conventional investments.

Like it or not, when we consider what we desire when we choose a place to live, we find that government affects most of the factors that affect our quality of life.

But, but, but . . . the conservatives say the private sector could do better much of what government does. To that I answer that our two of our largest federal agencies, the Social Security Administration and Medicare, have more efficient administrations than comparable organizations in the private sector.

A few examples of government efficiency are not likely to dissuade those who believe that for-profit organizations are inherently more efficient and effective than public ones. My contention is that inefficiency and ineffectiveness can occur in any organization, public or private. To bolster my case, I told the story of two widely admired, innovative US companies, Xerox and General Electric. Xerox became efficient, appeared to lose that efficiency, and regained it a second time. General Electric became highly efficient over a period of many years. Jack Welch alludes to the usual state of an organization in the following excerpt from his letter to shareholders in GE's 2000 annual report. This was written after his company had saved billions of dollars over several years by improving internal processes:

> "We cultivate the hatred of bureaucracy in our Company and never for a moment hesitate to use that awful word "hate." Bureaucrats must be ridiculed and removed. They multiply in organizational layers and behind functional walls—which means that every day must be a battle to demolish this structure and keep the organization open, ventilated and free. Even if bureaucracy is largely exterminated, as it has been at GE, people need to be vigilant—even paranoid—because the allure of bureaucracy is part of human nature and hard to resist, and it can return in the blink of an eye. Bureaucracy frustrates people, distorts their priorities, limits their dreams and turns the face of the entire enterprise inward."[3]

Bureaucracy abounds in the land, and not just in the public sector. Private organizations become efficient and productive only when they must to survive, or when the likes of Jack Welch serve as leaders. The information I offer about public and for-profit organizations is, admittedly, anecdotal. But it should be enough to establish doubt about the conventional wisdom concerning the inherent superiority of one over the other. What has been said of improvement in private organizations can be said for public ones. Those who study organizational behavior would agree that an organization is an organization is an organization.

I briefly describe the use of quality methodology, six sigma and lean systems to improve an organization's efficiency. These, I believe, are the best means, although not the only ones, for improving an organization's efficiency. The best improvements require investment in training, and, these days, information technology. Starving an organization of funds is not likely to produce optimal results.

Those who want government to do less may not want to be reminded that the Clinton administration made headway in creating a government that worked better and cost less. For those of us who don't share the right's desire to reduce government function but who want the best use made of our tax dollars, Clinton's initiatives are impressive. Led by Vice President Al Gore, the National Performance Review based its work on four principles of "putting customers first, cutting red tape, empowering employees, and cutting back to basics."[4] The first four years of the initiative yielded "an overall reduction of 291,000 positions and savings of about $118 billion. In addition, agencies cut 640,000 pages of internal regulations (equivalent to 130 cases of copy paper) and created and publicly committed to meeting 3,500 customer service standards. Regulatory agencies cut regulations affecting the public by nearly 16,000 pages and rewrote another 31,000 pages to make them more understandable."[5] In recent decades it has been the Democratic administrations, those of Clinton and Carter, that initiated reforms to make government more efficient and responsive.

David Osborne, whose work was an "intellectual guidepost" for the Clinton administration's reinvention of government, has studied government reform abroad. New Zealand and Great Britain have "leaped far ahead of the United States into what they call 'the new public management.'"[6] Whether one endorses changes in these countries or not, lessons learned have relevance to us: "In 1988, New Zealand did away with its rule-bound civil service system, while preserving its protections against political interference in hiring and firing. Several years later, the United Kingdom let agencies radically simplify their personnel rules. Both countries have enjoyed excellent results, with few problems." New Zealand reduced its core public sector from 88,000 employees in 1987 to 32,000 in 2000.

The shrinking of the public sector in New Zealand (and in the U.K.) has not weakened the state; it has strengthened it. "It turns out that smaller governments are sometimes stronger governments, because they are more effective. Majorities of citizens abroad, as in the United States, no longer want big, bureaucratic government—but that doesn't mean they want minimalist government. Instead, they want lean, activist government that solves problems with as little waste and bureaucracy as possible."[7]

One of the many measures taken was to separate "steering" (policy and direction) from "rowing (service delivery and compliance enforcement)" and "walling off the rowing agencies behind more effective barriers to political manipulation." Another was to hand over "dramatic flexibilities" in return for "serious accountability." Managers are given "up to a dozen clear, measurable performance targets. If they meet most or all of them, they are eligible for bonuses of around 10 percent of their salaries. If they consistently fail, they may find themselves out of work." Osborne believes that as we struggle to overcome the limits of rule-driven bureaucracy, "We are gradually redesigning our public systems, to create adaptive, decentralized institutions capable of producing continuous improvement."[8] Those in the private sector will recognize these as first-rate management practices. Government can do it as well as the private sector.

One of the improvements endorsed by Osborne is outsourcing. There is plenty of well-documented savings in the public sector from outsourcing, but there, as in the private sector, cost savings is not a slam dunk. Outsourcing benefits an organization by relieving it of non-core functions, providing it with expertise, and improving service. And some types of outsourcing or privatizing may continue to save costs. But in 2002 and 2003, federal government employees won 75 percent and 89 percent of sourcing competitions, respectively. If these kinds of results continue, competitions should be suspended, because they are costly. Conservative hopes of substantially reducing government cost by hiring the private sector may have to be abandoned. President Reagan's assertion that "government does nothing as well or as economically as the private sector" is already open to question. An organization is an organization is an organization.

Faith in outsourcing and in the efficiency of for-profit organizations is understandable if questionable at this point. It has been the conventional wisdom for many, many years. Not understandable is the Right's lack of concern about government contracts going to those who repeatedly break the law, engage in other misbehavior, or fail to make their tax payments. Raising little or no objection to the government rehiring contractors with such bad track records is mystifying. Yes, the companies pay penalties to the government when misbehavior is apprehended. But that's it. All the while the Right complains that the government bureaucracy is inherently unaccountable. This tendentious lack of concern leaves the Right open to suspicions that they will support the for-profit sector come what may.

If contractor misbehavior is tolerated, can cronyism be far behind? With large and increasing amounts of government work going to contractors, cronyism is an increasing risk. We haven't heard about many examples, but with many thousands of government contracts in existence, we can be concerned that it already goes on without our knowledge. The tales of Halliburton misdeeds, waste, and suspicious billings involving contracts in Iraq may foreshadow future problems.

Cronyism appeared solidly in the saddle of Paul Bremer's Coalition Provisional Authority (CPA) in Iraq, according to a *Washington Monthly* report in December of 2003.[9] Bremer commandeered one of Saddam's Republican Palaces, and journalists found the venue aptly named. It seems that when hiring for the CPA began, State Department employees were excluded because State had resisted the hawks over Iraq strategy and were thought to be disloyal. Also excluded was anyone who had worked for an NGO or for the Clinton administration on the grounds they would be "ideologically suspect." Few with the requisite experience were either hired or consulted about hiring. Those hired were "card–carrying Republicans—operatives, flacks, policy–wonks and lobbyists—for almost every key assignment in the country." One official said, "They're trying to do the right thing, but they do what they do without any knowledge of how the post-war world works in reality. But what is clear is that they know nothing about development, and nothing about transitional economies." The *Washington Monthly* suggests when the dust settles in Iraq, historians may find the CPA's lack of experience just might have contributed to the post-invasion's descent in chaos and disorder. If the *Monthly* is correct, then the price for this instance of cronyism will be very, very steep.

Another concern is inadequate protection for government employees when reforms are implemented. If civil service is replaced, employees must be protected from political manipulation as well as arbitrary removal. That is one of the lessons Osborne drew from the experiences of New Zealand and the U.K.[10] But the State of Florida's reforms have left many employees feeling quite vulnerable. In 2001, Florida's Governor Jeb Bush signed into law a "sweeping civil service overhaul package."[11] Florida became one of only three states (Texas and Georgia are the other two) to "substantially eliminate civil service protection for executive-branch employees." Two concerns have arisen: "First, it exposes state workers who enforce regulations and license businesses and professionals to the risk of retribution for pursuing cases against politically well-connected Floridians. Second, it leaves higher-salaried senior staff exposed to the whims of departmental budget cutters who, like a sports-team owner trying to meet a salary cap, might be tempted to off-load more senior, high-paid staff just to save money, regardless of what it means by way of institutional brain drain or employee morale."

There is no shortage of whistleblowers in Florida who claim they were fired for political reasons or because they took regulatory action against a friend of the governor. They have a website called Whose Florida.[12] One of the most blatant developments was the exclusion of three occupational groups from the new, flexible personnel regimen: police, fire fighters and, curiously, dietitians. What might these three groups have in common? Their unions endorsed Governor Bush in 1998! Many other awards of government contracts to friends of Jeb Bush have been alleged, a charge he consistently denies.

Conservative views on the needy appear in Chapter 6. I demonstrate that it is quite unrealistic to expect the private sector to take over support for those on limited incomes. If conservatives have their way and government budgets are lowered even more, then we can expect even less from the private sector. The needs of low income citizens will have to compete with even more causes. New organizations that support schools, for example, have begun to raise funds not for the traditional school extras such as field trips or band uniforms, but for core needs such as teachers. And, sad to say, National Guard reservists fundraise for adequate equipment to fight the war on terror.

Some on the right have high expectations for faith-based initiatives as a way of addressing the needs of low-income citizens. One cannot read about these projects without being immensely impressed by the dedication of faith volunteers who work in prisons or in poor inner-city neighborhoods to help those that seem to be abandoned and without hope. Faith-based initiatives have already proven that they can get good results. Whether their results will be better than those of secular organizations remains to be seen. Although they may attribute their successes to faith, sustained personal attention to those whom they help is likely to be a strong factor as well.

In recognizing the dedication of faith-based volunteers I do not disregard, as do some of their ranks, the enormous contribution made by millions of other volunteers in our society. I share the discomfort of many who bristle at this new cozy relationship between agents of faith and agents of government. There is, however, more than plenty of work to go around for both secular and faith-based organizations. We just must be certain that outcome studies measure the effects of these organizations to be sure that the blurring of religion and state boundaries is justified by superior results.

One of the recent difficulties experienced in secular volunteering—and suggested in some of the faith-based literature I have read as well—is a worsening shortage of volunteers willing to provide help over a sustained period. Diane Brady, executive director of the Volunteer Resource Center of the Twin Cities said recently, "People's availability has changed. Volunteers are looking increasingly for short-term episodic commitments. As lives become increasingly busy . . . potential volunteers have less time to give." She sees this as a major national trend at the same time that many nonprofit groups "absolutely depend on volunteers."[13] Big Brothers Big Sisters in the Twin Cities, for example, has a "huge waiting list." On the average, girls have a three month wait; boys wait nine months.

With such shortages, might the for-profit sector, encouraged after taking on some traditionally public institutions, be the next player in this area? Paid volunteers? In a competition between a faith-based organization and a for-profit one, how would we decide?

We might have something to learn about volunteering from the Europeans. Really. Lester Salamon has been studying the non-profit world for many years. In a recent article he described the upswing of volunteerism in countries outside the U.S.[14] The highest rates of volunteerism,[15] occur in Sweden followed by the Netherlands, Norway and the United States. France and the U.K followed. Salamon concluded that volunteering tends to be greatest in countries with high levels of non-profit paid employment. And the higher the level of government spending, the more extensive volunteering is. Volunteering does not compete with government spending. "Rather," he concludes, "they spring from the same sentiments of generosity, solidarity and caring."

One of the concerns many of us to the left of center have about the conservatives is what appears to be a retreat from caring for those in need. Of course, right wingers don't acknowledge this; we are told instead about compassionate conservatism. And those who tell us about it are smiling, congenial politicians who don't look like they could be unkind to anyone. So we have a hard time comprehending what we hear or read about their reduction of funds to the economically disadvantaged in our society.

Reduced caring for the poor appears in what seems to be a reasonable redefinition of poverty: The poor are not penniless. In chapter 7, I described examples of this attitude in legislation passed in Minnesota in 2003. Those depending on medical assistance must provide a nominal co-payment for their medications and certain medical services, and those charged with a crime must pay a fee, which could not be waived, for public defense services. Legislators were probably thinking of that group of needy citizens they usually think about when poverty is discussed: young, single adults. They were not thinking about the mentally or physically disabled or the frail elderly, who when ill, could easily be penniless when they need to fill a prescription.

Another claim heard on the right is that the poor are far better off than they used to be. The message, always implicit, of course is that we don't have to feel quite as sorry for them as we thought. A chapter in Julian Simon's text, *The State of Humanity*[16] asks, "How 'Poor' are America's Poor?" In it we are reminded that the poor (along with the rest of us) didn't have running water, flush toilets, or electric lights at the beginning of the century. The poor and the rest of us should be more appreciative. Yes, the poor, along with the rest of us, are better off. Our middle class lives more comfortably than aristocrats used to live. And our wealthy, even without a retinue of servants, lives like royalty. The chapter goes on to point out the other things that many of the poor have now: automobiles, air conditioning, refrigerators, washing machines microwave ovens, and telephones (Why televisions were left off the list is a mystery).

The prices of many of the gadgets of our time are quite low, and they are even lower on the second-hand market. What is left out of this story is that the low prices that benefit all of us have resulted from global competition and immigrant labor. But when an item is not subject to these market forces, it becomes unaffordable to the poor. We would like the poor, who are able, to keep up with current events. They can buy a television for well under a $100 new and a used one for well under $50. But the better source of information would be a newspaper. The pricing of newspapers is not affected by global competition. So annual subscriptions can run between $100 to $200 or more—as much as a bunch of used television sets.

But the more important example of something whose price does not reflect foreign competition—that is constructed with the wages of American labor and with prices of American materials—is the greatest living cost of all, housing. Even after years into a real estate boom, affordable housing for those with modest and low incomes is as difficult to come by as it has been for several decades. What has happened in the last decade is that the poor now share this serious problem with teachers, firefighters, police officers, nurses and hospital workers. The Bank of America and Fannie Mae (Federal National Mortgage Association) are teaming up to assist individuals in these occupations with home financing.[17] The poor, who do not already have affordable housing, put their names on waiting lists and commonly wait for years. In the area of housing, the free enterprise system is serving fewer and fewer citizens.

If the right has its way, it will not only be the poor who will be adversely affected. It is the right's agenda to dismantle the ideas and programs of Roosevelt's New Deal, and privatize much of what government now does. Those who have and create wealth will be become even more favored. Everyone else will be offered heavy doses of the American Dream and family values. That will mean that a small percent of our population will be denied the rights to marry. A second Bush term will certainly change the composition of the Supreme Court, and that increases the likelihood that another small percentage of us will not be able to obtain an abortion. Most of us will not be personally affected by these changes, but those who support these values will have a feeling that the state of the nation is in a better place. We will be offered a new trade off: fewer benefits and more values. If it comes to this, will Americans feel grateful or feel like suckers?

In the twentieth century we traded part of our incomes for education, highways, better health, consumer protection, help for the needy, and many other things. I have argued that our taxes and our government helped expand our freedoms, enhance our wealth, and improve our quality of life. And I have provided evidence to show numerous flaws in the conservative assumptions about taxes and government. Their case has lots of cracks.

Appendix I

Calculation of an upper limit of charitable giving to the economically disadvantaged for the year 2000

The categories of charitable giving reported in the *Statistical Abstract of the United States*[1] do not easily yield information about giving to the needy in our society. Portions of some contain the needed data. For example the category of "Human Service" includes emergency food and clothing assistance. No philanthropic categories (and very few of the sub-categories not reported in the Statistical Abstract) list organizations that benefit low-income people exclusively.

Even within a category like Human Services, extracting charity to the needy from charity for other purposes is nearly impossible. Instead, one can make informed decisions about which portions include giving to the needy and include those portions in their entirety. I examine each category to find the smallest components in which giving to the needy occur. In this way I include much more than we should, but include all that we need. For example, the United Way provides many funds to the economically disadvantaged, but also helps those of average means. If we include all United Way giving, then we can say that actual giving to the needy is below this value.* We will have to plead ignorance about just how much below this calculated maximum actual giving is. The result I derive, an upper limit of giving, will be useful for the purposes of this project.

In the following analysis I assume that the proportion of giving within a category varies little over the course of a few years, and that published studies of a portion of givers (details presented below) are representative of all givers in the category.

Data from Table 6.3, including additional information is reproduced in Table A.1 along with a brief description of the charitable categories to be analyzed.[2] Some portion of the categories in italics benefits the economically disadvantaged.

A portion of contributions to religious causes serves the needy. These funds go by various names, as shown in Table A.2.

The lack of uniformity in nomenclature used by congregations to describe giving outside of their walls is matched by a lack of uniformity in practice. It is not uncommon for congregational giving to occur outside church budgets. Such contributions are counted as individual giving. For that reason the amounts contributed by U.S. congregations to the needy are very approximate. Nevertheless, Table A.2 does reveal that total contributions outside the local church are fairly uniform, between approximately 11 percent and 16 percent. This observation is consistent with that of Hoge et al, "In the mid-1990s, an average of 10 to 15 percent of all contributions are being spent on missions outside the local church, . . ."[13] Cnaan's higher percent is consistent with his inclusion of items not usually associated with caring for the needy, such as music performances, holiday celebrations, community bazaars and fairs, and choral groups. These activities would go on whether or not

---

*Another way to describe this process is to say that we will take away all portions of charitable giving that do not include funds for the needy and add up what remains.

Table A.1
Categories and Amounts of Private Philanthropic Giving in 2000

Destination of funds	Types of organizations included[3]	Dollars Contributed (in billions)
Religion	Houses of worship, national headquarters of faith traditions, missionary societies	$77.0
Education	Universities, K-12	$31.7
Health	Support for named diseases, health facilities, research, and others	$18.8
Human services	Basic needs, youth development or care, emergency relief and the like	$18.0
Arts, culture, humanities		$11.5
Public-society benefit	United Way and other charities that make gifts to other non-profit groups, community development organizations, research facilities and other groups	$11.6
Environment, wildlife		$6.2
International		$3.7
Gifts to foundations	Public society benefit, education, human services, arts, culture and the like	$24.7
Unallocated	Not assigned to a category	$25.2

Table A.2
Summary of studies on donations by U. S. congregations that includes help to the economically disadvantaged

Description of donation likely to include help for the needy	Percent of church expenditures	Study Source
Donations to denominational and nondenominational organizations and direct assistance to individuals	To denominational organizatons, 10 percent, to nondenominational organizations and direct assistance to individuals, 4 percent	Sample of U.S. congregations conducted by INDEPENDENT SECTOR in 1992 [4]
Donations to denominational and nondenominational organizations and direct assistance to individuals	To denominational organizations 8 percent, to nondenominational organizations and direct assistance to individuals, 4 percent	Sample of US congregations conducted by INDEPENDENT SECTOR in 1996 [5]
Donations to denominational and nondenominational organizations and direct assistance to individuals	9 percent	L. M. Salamon's conclusion about data from INDEPENDENT SECTOR'S 1992 study, see above [6]
Total missions	15 percent	Sample of *Christianity Today* subscribers (Evangelical Protestant) in 2001 [7]
Denominational and other missions	10.7 percent to 15.7 percent	Samples of one Catholic and four Protestant denominations [8]

Benevolences as a percentage of total contributions reported for various years, 1996 through 2002	15 percent	Yearbook of American and Canadian Churches 2003[9]
Social ministry, including international relief	17.4 percent	113 historic churches, all built before 1940[10]
Social service expenditures	3 percent	From National Congregations Study, a sample of U.S. congregations, 1998[11]
Missions, international and domestic	Total missions 16 percent, international 9 percent, domestic 7 percent	Sample of U.S. congregations commissioned by Christianity Today International in 2000[12]

the needy were present. Non-members who attend might be individuals with low incomes, but that is not necessarily the case.

Unfortunately (for our purposes) the portion that congregations contribute to their own denominations can contain a portion which is given to charitable projects.[14] Therefore we cannot use the denominational vs. nondenominational distinction to estimate charitable giving to the needy. Salamon's figure of nine percent is based upon what he considers to be reasonable assumptions. Two of the studies, the last two in Table A.2, define giving in a way that is useful for our purpose. Both of the studies sampled U.S. congregations. One asked about international and domestic missions, and the other asked about social service spending. Since an upper limit is being calculated, we will use the higher of the two studies, 7 percent of expenditures. This estimate of the upper limit of giving to the needy does not contradict the other studies, because many of them include international missions and domestic missions which have other purposes such as evangelism.

The Human Service category includes organizations devoted to recreation and sports, youth, traditional social services to the needy such as emergency assistance, and others.[15] The American Red Cross and organizations with a religious connection that provide social services, such as Catholic Charities, are included in this category.

It is likely that a substantial portion of funds in the Human Service category goes to the needy. The 2003 edition of Giving USA,[16] reports on the amount and percentage given to Human Services in 2000 by 66 organizations that raised $20 million or more (totaling $4.73 billion). We will use the proportions in this study as representative of all giving to Human Service: "Basic needs" and "Youth development or care" each received 33 percent of the total; "Emergency relief" received 11 percent; and the "Other" category (which includes services to promote the independence of special populations) received 6 percent. The total of these sub-categories is 83 percent of all Human Services giving. (Categories not included were "Credit counseling," "Amateur sports," and Fundraising for human services.")

What can be said for the Human Services category is true to a lesser degree for the category of Public-Society Benefit. This category includes contributions to organizations who in turn distribute funds to other agencies. Organizations in this category include the United Way campaigns, Combined Federal Campaign (a fund comparable to the United Way but which operates in the Federal workplace), United Jewish Appeal, and others.[17] We will depend on a study of the 125 public society benefit organizations that raised $20 million or more in 2000.[18] Of the Public-Society Benefit category, we include the entire contributions to United Way (25 percent), other grant making or giving organizations (34 percent), one-fourth of Jewish community fundraising (4.6 percent),[19] and funds going to veterans (2 percent). Summing these percentages, we conclude that at most, 66 percent of Public-Society Benefit contributions go to the needy.

Overall, U.S. philanthropic contributions to Education are second in size only to those given to Religion. The Council for Aid to Education/RAND estimates that a little over 80 percent of education contributions are given to U.S. colleges and universities.[20] We can make an estimate of what portion of the Education category could benefit those with low incomes from a study of the contributions of 108 educational organizations that raised $20 million or more (for a total of $5.0 billion) in the year 2000.[21] The portion of this giving likely to benefit low-income students is scholarships comprising 8 percent of the total. We know that not all scholarships are targeted to the needy, so the 8 percent quoted provides an upper limit of giving.

Most of the contributions in the Health category support health facilities or activities, such as research related to a disease or a disorder. According to data from 98 health organizations that raised $20 million or more for a total of $6.1 billion in 2000, 48 percent went to health facilities and 42 percent to support for named diseases, disorders or conditions.[22] The 1999 edition of *Giving USA* quotes an Association for Healthcare Philanthropy study on the $5.71 billion contributed in 1998 saying that 9 percent of the contributions to healthcare organizations are used for charitable care.[23] We will estimate that 9 percent of the 48 percent contributed to health facilities or 4.3 percent of all Health contributions go to the needy.

In the year 2000 foundations gave away $24.7 billion in grants. The Foundation Center provides statistical studies on grants designated by population group[24] and by subject categories.[25] An estimate of foundation giving to the needy was made using both studies. In 2000 16.4 percent of designated grants were granted to the economically disadvantaged and 3.2 percent went to the disabled. If we assume that the same percentages of the grants that were not designated or went to the general public (62 percent) went to the needy, we add another 12 percent for a total of 32 percent. Alternatively, a determination by subject categories can be made using estimates we have already derived. We assume the same percentages of grants were given to Health (4.3 percent) and Education (8 percent) categories as were donated by all givers. From the Human Services category of 14.4 percent of all foundation giving, we subtract only the "recreation and sport" sub-category of 1.4 percent. From the Public-Society Benefit category of 11.3 percent we subtract only the sub-category of "public affairs," of 2.6 percent. Adding all category estimates, we come to a total of 34 percent, very close to the 32 percent we calculated based on the statistics for populations served. Since we have been choosing maximum values, we use the 34 percent value.

The upper limit estimates appear in the following table. It was assumed that the same proportion of unallocated funds went to the needy as those funds that were allocated.

Table A3.
Calculated Upper Limit of Philanthropic giving in 2000 to the economically disadvantaged

Destination of funds contributed	Total contributions (in billions)	Giving to the needy equals or is less than	Estimated upper limit of giving (billions)
Religion	$77.4	7 percent	$5.42
Education	$31.7	8 percent	$2.54
Health	$18.8	4.3 percent	$0.81
Human services	$18.0	83 percent	$14.9
Arts, culture, humanities	$11.5		0
Public-society benefit	$11.6	66 percent	$7.66
Environment, wildlife	$6.2		0
International	$3.7		0
Gifts to foundations	$24.7	34 percent	$8.52
Total allocated funds	$203.1	20 percent	$39.85
Unallocated	$25.2	20 percent	$4.94
TOTAL	**$228.3**		**$44.80**

Notes

NOTES TO CHAPTER TWO

1. Moody, J. Scott and Scott A. Hodge, April 2003 and April 2004, "America Celebrates Tax Freedom Day," Tax Foundation, http://www.taxfoundation.org/sr129.pdf (accessed August 7, 2004)
2. Moody, J. Scott and Scott A. Hodge, April 2003, see above
3. Moody, J. Scott and Scott A. Hodge, April 2003, see above
4. Moody, J. Scott and Scott A. Hodge, April 2003, see above
5. During much of the century a closely related quantity, gross national product (GNP) was used. It is used in this chart when GDP was not available. For our purposes, they are identical.
6. GDP and GNP data from Bureau of Economic Analysis, http://www.bea.gov/bea/dn/nipaweb/index.asp (accessed August 7, 2004) and *Historical Statistics of the United States, Colonial Times to 1970, Bicentennial edition*, 1975, Washington D.C., U.S Department of Commerce, Bureau of the Census
7. Caplow, Theodore, Louis Hicks, and Ben J. Wattenberg, 2001, *The First Measured Century—An Illustrated Guide to Trends in America 1900–2000*, Washington D.C., The AEI Press
8. US Patent and Trademark Office. "U.S. Patent Activity—Calendar Years 1790-2001," http://www.uspto.gov/web/offices/ac/ido/oeip/taf/h_counts.htm (Accessed August 7, 2004)
9. GDP and GNP data from Bureau of Economic Analysis, and *Historical Statistics of the United States, Colonial Times to 1970, Bicentennial edition*, 1975, see above

130 *Cracks in the Foundation*

10. GDP and GNP data from Bureau of Economic Analysis, and *Historical Statistics of the United States, Colonial Times to 1970, Bicentennial edition*, 1975, see above
11. Miles, Marc A., Edwin J. Feulner, Jr., Mary Anastasia O'Grady, and Ana I. Eiras, 2004, "2004 Index of Economic Freedom: Establishing the Link between Economic Freedom and Prosperity" The Heritage Foundation and Dow Jones & Company, Inc. http://www.heritage.org/research/features/index/ (accessed July 31, 2004)
12. O'Grady, Mary Anastasia, "Free Markets, Free People," *The Wall Street Journal*, January 9, 2004
13. Miles, Marc A., Edwin J. Feulner, Jr., Mary Anastasia O'Grady, and Ana I. Eiras, 2004, see above
14. The Organization for Economic Cooperation and Development, OECD, has 30 member countries and "relationships with some 70 other countries, NGOs and civil society." Members share "a commitment to democratic government and the market economy." "Best known for its publications and its statistics, its work covers economic and social issues from macroeconomics, to trade, education, development and science and innovation." Website: http://www.oecd.org/ accessed July 31, 2004) Data quoted is from OECD's "Revenue Statistics 1965-2001," 2002 http://www.oecd.org/dataoecd/6/63/1962227.pdf (accessed August 7, 2004)

NOTES TO CHAPTER THREE

1. Heston Alan, Robert Summers and Bettina Aten, October 2002, "Penn World Table Version 6.1," Center for International Comparisons at the University of Pennsylvania (CICUP), http://www.pwt.econ.upenn.edu/php_site/pwt_index.php (accessed July 31, 2004)
2. Wehrfritz, George and Alexandra A. Seno, March 29, 2004, "Turning Japanese?" *Newsweek International*, Atlantic Edition
3. The Organization for Economic Cooperation and Development (OECD). For description see footnote 14, in chapter 2. Data quoted is from OECD, 2002, "Revenue Statistics 1965-2001," http://www.oecd.org/dataoecd/6/63/1962227.pdf (accessed August 7, 2004)
4. International Monetary Fund (IMF) The IMF is an organization of 184 countries, working to foster global monetary cooperation, secure financial stability, facilitate international trade, promote high employment and sustainable economic growth, and reduce poverty.

5. Unless stated otherwise, only nations whose economic data was available for the year 1999 or 2000 were included. The caveats concerning the measurement of tax burden noted in Chapter 2 are applicable here as well. With international comparisons, differing governmental accounting systems add an additional degree of uncertainty. For the tax burden calculation, OECD includes all taxes while IMF includes only taxes collected from the central government. Therefore, for countries outside the OECD, state or province and local taxes were added to central government taxes to calculate tax burden. Additional data obtained from "Government Finance Statistics Yearbook," 2002, Vol. XXV, Washington D.C., International Monetary Fund, and "International Financial Statistics Yearbook," Vol. LIV, Washington D.C., International Monetary Fund
6. The World Factbook, http://www.odci.gov/cia/publications/factbook/ (accessed July 31, 2004)
7. Miles, Marc A., Edwin J. Feulner, Jr., Mary Anastasia O'Grady, and Ana I. Eiras, 2004, "2004 Index of Economic Freedom: Establishing the Link between Economic Freedom and Prosperity" The Heritage Foundation and Dow Jones & Company, Inc. http://www.heritage.org/research/features/index/ (accessed July 31, 2004)
8. OECD, "Total expenditure on health, % GDP," http://www.oecd.org/dataoecd/13/13/31963469.xls (accessed July 31, 2004)
9. Derived from Hong Kong government statistics at http://www.info.gov.hk/yearbook/2001/ehtml/appendices/app-14.htm and http://www.info.gov.hk/censtatd/eng/statliteracy/edu_booklet/introtogdp/gdpgnpbop.htm (accessed August 7, 2004)
10. Heston Alan, Robert Summers and Bettina Aten, October 2002, see above
11. Heston Alan, Robert Summers and Bettina Aten, October 2002, see above. GDP values in Figure 3.1 are from a chained series, an adjustment calculated to improve comparison with the previous and following years, and, therefore, differ from values in Tables 3.1, 3.2, and 3.3.

NOTES TO CHAPTER FOUR

1. *Historical Statistics of the United States, Colonial Times to 1970, Bicentennial edition*, 1975, Washington, D.C., Bureau of the Census, U.S. Department of Commerce
2. *Historical Statistics of the United States, Colonial Times to 1970, Bicentennial edition*, 1975, see above

3. From Erie Canal online, http://www.syracuse.com/features/eriecanal/intro.html (accessed August 8, 2004)
4. Cox, Wendell and Jean Love, June 1996, "40 Years of the US Interstate Highway System: An Analysis—The Best Investment A Nation Ever Made," http://www.publicpurpose.com/freeway1.htm (accessed August 8, 2004)
5. Schrank, D. L. and T. J. Lomax, September 2003, "2003 Annual Urban Mobility Report," http://tti.tamu.edu/product/product_details.asp?book_id=27290 (accessed August 8, 2004) The Texas Transportation Institute is the nation's largest university-affiliated transportation research agency.
6. The American Society of Civil Engineers ""Report Card for America's Infrastructure, 2003 Progress Report—An Update to the 2001 Report Card" http://www.asce.org/reportcard/index.cfm (accessed August 8, 2004)
7. The ASCE did note an improvement in the percent of structurally deficient bridges over the previous two years: 27.5% of the nation's bridges (162,000) in 2000 compared to 29% in 1998.
8. *Historical Statistics of the United States, Colonial Times to 1970, Bicentennial edition,* Series 599, Bureau of the Census, U.S. Department of Commerce, 1975
9. *Historical Statistics of the United States, Colonial Times to 1970, Bicentennial edition,* Series 599, see above
10. "Percent of People 25 Years and Over Who Have Completed High School or College, by Race, Hispanic Origin and Sex: Selected Years 1940 to 2003," http://www.census.gov/population/socdemo/education/tabA-2.xls (accessed August 8, 2004)
11. The Morrill Act of 1862, which led to the formation of the "land grant" universities.
12. Light, Paul C., 2002, *Government's greatest achievements: from civil rights to homeland defense*, Washington, D.C., The Brookings Institution
13. Caplow, Theodore, Louis Hicks, and Ben J. Wattenberg, 2001, *The First Measured Century, An Illustrated Guide to Trends in America, 1900–2000,* Washington, D.C. The AEI Press
14. Website: http://www.nsf.gov/home/about/creation.htm (accessed August 8, 2004)
15. Website: http://www.darpa.mil/ (accessed August 8, 2004)
16. Light, Paul C, 2002, see above
17. Leviticus 19:35
18. Magill, Frank N., editor, 1994, *Great Events from History,* Volume II, Business and Commerce Series, Pasadena, CA, Salem Press, Inc.

19. The Consumer Product Safety Commission website, http://www.cpsc.gov/about/about.html (accessed August 8, 2004)
20. "The SEC: Who We Are, What We Do," http://www.sec.gov/about/whatwedo.shtml (accessed August 8, 2004)
21. "The SEC: Who We Are, What We Do," see above
22. *The Bond Buyer*, March 22, 2000 v331 i30854 p5 and *Fund Action*, Feb 14, 2000 v11 i7 p9
23. *San Jose Mercury News*, Jan. 15, 2003, editorial
24. Kurian, George T., 1994, *Datapedia of the United States, 1790–2000*, Latham, MD, Bernan Press
25. Kurian, George T., 1994, see above
26. NIH website: http://www.nih.gov/about/NIHoverview.html (accessed August 8, 2004)
27. Light, Paul C, 2002, see above
28. Rolnick, Art, and Grunewald, Rob, Dec. 2003, "Early Childhood Development: Economic Development with a High Public Return," The Region, Vol 17, No 4 supplement, Federal Reserve Bank of Minneapolis
29. References used for finding an ideal place to live are: Savageau, David and Ralph D'Agostino, 2000, *Places Rated Almanac: Your Guide to Finding the Best Places to Live in North America*, Rand McNally, and Morgan, Kathleen O'Leary and Scott Morgan, editors, "State Rankings 2004—14th Annual Most Livable State," 15th edition, Lawrence, KS, Morgan Quitno at http://www.morganquinto.com/
30. Morgan, Kathleen O'Leary and Scott Morgan, editors, "State Rankings 2004—14th Annual Most Livable State" see above
31. American Lung Association, April 29, 2004, "State of the Air: 2004" http://www.lungusa.org/ (accessed August 8, 2004)
32. *The Gallup Poll 2000*, 2001, Wilmington, DE, The Gallup Organization, Scholarly Resources
33. The complete texts of these speeches and much more about the Marshall Plan can be found at http://www.usaid.gov/multimedia/video/marshall/ (accessed August 8, 2004)
34. Marshall Plan website, see above
35. From a brief history of the National Park Service, http://www.cr.nps.gov/history/hisnps/NPSHistory/npshisto.htm (accessed August 8, 2004)

NOTES TO CHAPTER FIVE

1. From Backgrounder on the Pendleton Act, http://usinfo.state.gov/usa/infousa/facts/democrac/28.htm (accessed August 2, 2004)
2. From 'LEADERS FOR A CHANGE', Jimmy Carter for President 1976 Campaign Brochure, at http://www.4president.org/ocmi1976.htm, (accessed August 2, 2004)
3. From "Ronald Reagan Legacy Project," http://www.reaganlegacy.org/speeches/reagan.torestore.3.31.76.htm (accessed August 2, 2004)
4. Light, Paul C., 2003, "Fact Sheet on the New True Size of Government," http://www.brook.edu/dybdocroot/gs/cps/light20030905.pdf , (accessed August 2, 2004)
5. Light, Paul C., 2003, see above
6. Social Security and Medicare Boards of Trustees, "Status of the Social Security and Medicare Programs, A summary of the 2004 Annual Reports" http://www.ssa.gov/OACT/TRSUM/trsummary.html (accessed August 2, 2004)
7. for example, Mitchell, Olivia S., 1998, "Administrative Costs in Public and Private Retirement Systems," in Martin Feldstein, ed., page 403, *Privatizing Social Security*, Chicago, IL, The University of Chicago Press
8. American Customer Satisfaction Index, http://www.theacsi.org/overview.htm (accessed August 2, 2004)
9. "Special Report: Government satisfaction scores," December 15, 2003, http://www.theacsi.org/government.htm (accessed August 2, 2004)
10. The American Customer Satisfaction Index, "Fourth Quarter Scores" February 18, 2004 http://www.theacsi.org/fourth_quarter.htm#ins1 (accessed August 2, 2004)
11. Fornell, Professor Claes, December 15, 2003, "ACSI commentary: Federal Government Scores" http://www.theacsi.org/government/govt-03c.html (accessed August 2, 2004)
12. The American Customer Satisfaction Index, http://www.theacsi.org/government/govt-03c.html and http://www.theacsi.org/fourth_quarter.htm#bro , see above (accessed August 2, 2004)
13. Woolhandler, Steffie, Terry Campbell, and David U Himmelstein, August 21, 2003, "Costs of Health Care Administration in the United States and Canada," *New England Journal of Medicine*, *349*:8, page 768
14. In an editorial in the same issue Henry Aaron, an economist at the Brookings In-

stitution, disagrees with the magnitude of the difference between the US and Canadian costs found in the study. He estimates an excess of $159 billion is spent in the US, still a formidable figure. See Aaron, Henry J., August 21, 2003, "The Costs of Health Care Administration in the United States and Canada—Questionable Answers to a Questionable Question," *New England Journal of Medicine, 349*:8, page 801. The more recent report of the Medicare Board of Trustees cited above in footnote 6 quotes administrative expenses to be 1.6 percent of total expenditures in 2003.

15. Petty, Priscilla, 1991, Executive Producer, "The Deming of America", Petty Consulting Productions video
16. Gabor, Andrea, 1990, *The Man Who Discovered Quality*, Times Books, Random House, New York and Toronto
17. For more information on the Baldridge award, see http://baldrige.nist.gov/ (accessed August 2, 2004)
18. Arner, Faith and Adam Aston, May 3, 2004, "How Xerox Got Up To Speed; Learning fast from GE Capital, it applied Lean Six Sigma 'with a vengeance,'" *Business Week*
19. "What is Six Sigma? The Roadmap to Customer Impact" http://www.ge.com/files/usa/en/commitment/quality/sixsigma.pdf (accessed August 2, 2004)
20. Slater, Robert, 1999, *Jack Welch and the GE Way—Management Insights and Leadership Secrets of the Legendary CEO*, New York, McGraw-Hill.
21. Letter to shareholders, 1998, GE Annual Report, http://www.ge.com/annual98/index.htm (accessed August 2, 2004)
22. Letter to shareholders, 2002, GE Annual Report http://www.ge.com/annual00/index.html (accessed August 2, 2004)
23. Attributed to William Rupp, MD & CEO of the Luther/Midelfort-Mayo Health System
24. Accenture, 2003, "Outsourcing in Government: Pathways to Value," http://www.accenture.com/xd/.asp?it=enweb&xd=industries%5Cgovernment%5Cinsights%5Coutsourcing_2003.xml (accessed August 8, 2004). A major player in outsourcing, Accenture based this report on a survey of twenty-three nations. It provides a valuable overview of outsourcing around the world.
25. Accenture, 2003, see above.
26. Getronics and CIO, 2002, "The CIO Agenda: Taking Care of Business—International

IT Leaders Target New Spending, Security and Outsourcing Initiatives in 2003," CXO Media, Inc. http://www.cio.com/sponsors/120102getronics/ (accessed August 8, 2004)

27. Matlus, Richard T., May 5, 2004, "Outsourcing to Control Cost" http://outsourcing.weblog.gartner.com/weblog/index.php?blogid=9. (accessed August 5, 2004) The research director goes on to say that, "Gartner does emphasize that outsourcers can help control cost over time," and provides an example of how that could happen.

28. Chi, Keon S., 2003, Arnold Perkins, and Heather Perkins, Trends in State Government Management, The Book of States, The Council of State Governments, Lexington KY

29. Office of Management and Budget, May 2004, "Competitive Sourcing—Report on Competitive Sourcing Results Fiscal Year 2003," Executive Office of the President http://www.whitehouse.gov/omb/pubpress/fy2004/cs_omb_647_report.pdf (accessed August 2, 2004)

30. General Accounting Office, February 2004, "Competitive Sourcing—Greater Emphasis Needed on Increasing Efficiency and Improving Performance" Report GAO-04-367. GAO has since changed its name to General Accountability Office.

31. Perlman, Ellen, December 2002, "When it comes to outsourcing technology, big is not necessarily beautiful." *Governing*, published by the Congressional Quarterly

32. Avant, Deborah, May 9, 2004, "What are Those Contractors Doing in Iraq?" *The Washington Post*

33. Project on Government Oversight, 2002, "Federal Contractor Misconduct: Failures of the Suspension and Debarment System" http://www.pogo.org/p/contracts/co-020505-contractors.html (accessed August 2, 2004)

34. Government Acccounting Office, February 2004, "Some DOD Contractors Abuse the Federal Tax System with Little Consequence," GAO-04-414T

35. Press release from office of Senator Norm Coleman, R-MN, May 5, 2004, "Coleman, Levin introduce legislation to prevent federal contracts with known tax cheats"

36. *Times—Picayune*, Apr 8, 2000, "Fixing our Juvenile System," [ORLEANS Edition] New Orleans, La.

37. Butterfield, Fox, Mar 16, 2000, "Privately Run Juvenile Prison in Louisiana Is Attacked for Abuse of 6 Inmates" *New York Times*

38. Butterfield, Fox, Mar 16, 2000, see above
39. Butterfield, Fox, Mar 16, 2000, see above
40. Butterfield, Fox, Mar 16, 2000, see above
41. Ritea, Steve, Apr 5, 2000, "Judge Orders Negotiations in Juvenile Jail Suit Young Inmates Allege Rapes, Routine Beatings," *Times—Picayune* [ORLEANS Edition], New Orleans, La.
42. The Geo Group's website: http://www.thegeogroupinc.com/ (accessed August 2, 2004)
43. From Wall Street Week with Fortune, June 11, 2004, http://www.pbs.org/wsw/tvprogram/20040611.html (accessed August 2, 2004)
44. Henry Levin, Teachers College, Columbia University, quoted in Frontline, 2003, "Public Schools, Inc." Produced by: John D. Tulenko. The early history of Edison Schools related here is based upon Frontline's narrative.
45. Frontline, 2003, "Public Schools, Inc." Produced by: John D. Tulenko
46. Woodall, Martha, Nov 13, 2003, "Edison Schools Shareholders Accept $174 Million Buyout." *The Philadelphia Inquirer Knight Ridder/Tribune Business News*
47. Snyder, Susan, June 10, 2004, "Philadelphia students improve test scores," *Philadelphia Inquirer,*
48. For more information see http://www.edisonschools.com/ (accessed August 2, 2004)

NOTES TO CHAPTER SIX

1. For example, Olasky, Marvin N., *The Tragedy of American Compassion*, Regnery Publishing, Inc. 1995, (originally published in 1992)
2. Lyons, Eugene, 1964, *Herbert Hoover A Biography*, Garden City, NY, Doubleday & Company, Inc.
3. "The American Relief Administration in Soviet Russia," Hoover Institution Library and Archives, http://www-hoover.stanford.edu/hila/ara.htm (accessed August 3, 2004)
4. *Statistical Abstract of the United States 2002*, Table 516, based on a study by the Congressional Research Service, November 19, 2001, "Cash and Noncash Benefits for Persons With Limited Income: Eligibility Rules, Recipient and Expenditure Data, FY 1998-FY2000, CRS Report RL31228

5. *Statistical Abstract of the United States 2003*, Table 581, Source: AAFRC Trust for Philanthropy, Center on Philanthropy at Indiana University, Indianapolis, IN
6. *Statistical Abstract of the United States 2003*, Table 581, see above
7. Categories of giving are coded according the National Taxonomy of Exempt Entities (NTEE)—Core Codes formulated by Foundation Center. Charitable contributions to the same groups who receive government aid might be constructed from NTEE categories, but has not, to my knowledge, been reported. See http://fdncenter.org/research/grants_class/index.html for more on NTEE coding (accessed August 3, 2004)
8. Congressional Budget Office, December 2002, "Effects of Allowing Nonitemizers to Deduct Charitable Contributions" http://www.cbo.gov/ftpdoc.cfm?index=4008&type=1 (accessed August 3, 2004)
9. Independent Sector, adopted March 2001, "INDEPENDENT SECTOR Policy Position on the Charitable Deduction for Nonitemizers," http://www.independentsector.org/programs/gr/NCDPosition.html, (accessed August 3, 2004)
10. Education and Research Foundation of The Better Business Bureau serving Metropolitan New York, July 2003, "An Analysis of Survey Response Information About Funds Raised and Services Provided by 9-11 Related Charities" at http://www.newyork.bbb.org/disasterrelief/911Rpt-7-2003.pdf (accessed August 3, 2004)
11. Association of Fund-Raising Distributors and Suppliers press release of April 17 2002, "Product Sales Buy Schools, Non-Profits Net $1.9 Billion" http://www.afrds.com/homeframe.html (accessed August 3, 2004)
12. Lewis, Nicole, August 21, 2003, "Making the Grade: Public Schools raise millions with sophisticated techniques," *The Chronicle for Philanthropy*.
13. Lewis, Nicole, August 21, 2003, see above
14. Lewis, Nicole, August 21, 2003, see above
15. FEMA Disaster Expenditures January 1, 1990 to December 31, 2003 http://www.fema.gov/library/df_6.shtm (accessed August 3, 2004)
16. American Red Cross Financial Overview 2002, page 13 at http://www.redcross.org/pubs/car02/02financials.pdf (accessed August 3, 2004)
17. Substance Abuse and Mental Health Services Administration, Office of Applied Studies, September, 1998, "Services Research Outcomes Study," DHHS Publication No. (SMA) 98-3177), Washington, D.C., U.S. Government Printing Office. This large-scale study looked at persons with many kinds of addiction and motivation in many

kinds of treatment facilities. The relationship cited here is only one of many found in the study.

18. Glazer, Sarah, , May 2001, "Faith Based Initiatives," *CQ Researcher*, Vol 11, No. 17, Congressional Quarterly.
19. Prisoner Fellowship Ministries website: http://www.pfm.org/ (accessed August 3, 2004)
20. Johnson, Byron R. and David B Larson, 2003, "The InnerChange Freedom Initiative, A Preliminary Evaluation of a Faith-Based Prison Program," Center for Research on Religion and Urban Civil Society, University of Pennsylvania. A copy of the report is available at the Manhatten Institute for Policy Research website http://www.manhattan-institute.org/innerchange.pdf (accessed August 3, 2004)
21. Big Brothers Big Sisters website: http://www.bbbsa.org/site/pp.asp?c=iuJ3JgO2F&b=14600 (accessed August 3, 2004)
22. Tierney, Joseph P. and Jean Baldwin Grossman with Nancy L. Resch, reissued September 2000, "Making a Difference – An Impact Study of Big Brothers Big Sisters" A Publication of Public/Private Ventures http://www.ppv.org/ppv/publications/assets/111_publication.pdf (accessed August 3, 2004)
23. Dilulio Jr., John J., Fall 2002, "The Three Faith Factors," *Public Interest*
24. Bauldry, Shawn, and Tracy A Hartmann, March 2004, "The Promise and Challenge of Mentoring High-Risk Youth: Findings from the National Faith-Based Initiative" A publication of Public/Private Ventures, http://www.ppv.org/ppv/publications/assets/171_publication.pdf (accessed August 3, 2004)
25. Johnson, Byron, 2002, "Objective Hope—Assessing the Effectiveness of Faith-Based Organizations: A Review of the Literature," Center for Research on Religion and Urban Civil Society, University of Pennsylvania, http://www.manhattan-institute.org/crrucs_objective_hope.pdf (accessed August 3, 2004) This work provides a good overview of the effect of faith on many kinds of problems.
26. Johnson, Byron, 2002, see above
27. Chaves, Mark, and William Tsitsos, Spring 2001, "Congregations and Social Services: What They Do, How They Do It, and With Whom," Nonprofit Sector Research Fund Working Paper Series, The Aspen Institute, Washington D.C.
28. Chaves, Mark, and William Tsitsos, Spring 2001, see above
29. Cnaan, Ram A. and Stephanie Boddie, 2002, *The invisible caring hand: American*

congregations and the provision of welfare, New York University Press, New York, New York

30. Cnaan, Ram A. and Stephanie Boddie, 2002, see above

NOTES TO CHAPTER SEVEN

1. Minnesota Department of Trade and Economic Development, December 2001, Business Tracking System, "Minnesota Business Start-up, Dissolutions, Expansions, and Contractions" http://www.deed.state.mn.us/facts/PDFs/Bts-1202.pdf (accessed August 5, 2004)
2. Morgan, Kathleen O'Leary and Morgan, Scott, editors, State Rankings 2004 — 14th Annual Most Livable State, 15th edition, Morgan Quitno, Lawrence, KS. Reports can be accessed at http://www.morganquinto.com/ (accessed August 5, 2004)
3. Morgan, Kathleen O'Leary and Morgan, Scott, editors, 12th Annual Healthiest State 2004, 12th edition, Morgan Quitno, Lawrence, KS. Reports can be accessed at http://www.morganquinto.com/ (accessed August 5, 2004)
4. National State Technology & Science Index Overall Index, 2004 http://www.milkeninstitute.org/pdf/nstech_index04.pdf (accessed August 5, 2004)
5. Points of Light Foundation press release, June 1, 2004, "Points of Light Foundation Announces State Volunteering Rates," http://www.pointsoflight.org/about/mediacenter/releases/2004/06-01a.cfm (accessed August 5, 2004)
6. Florida, Richard, 2002, *The Rise of the Creative Class*, paperback edition, New York, NY Basic Books
7. United Way State of Caring Index for the Nation and the 50 States, http://national.unitedway.org/stateofcaring/view.cfm? (accessed August 5, 2004)
8. Robert Huggins Associates, "World Knowledge Competitiveness Index 2003," Wales, UK, http://www.hugginsassociates.com/index.php/cPath/22 (accessed August 5, 2004)
9. Shah, Allie, May 14, 2004, "'U' faculty salaries rank near bottom," *Star Tribune*
10. Taxpayers League of Minnesota, "We Proudly Present Our "No New Taxes" Pledge Signers," http://www.taxpayersleague.org/signers.php (accessed August 5, 2004)
11. Taxpayers League of Minnesota press release, March 8, 2004, "What Good Is It Anyway" http://www.taxpayersleague.org/issues/pr_display.php?rid=193 (accessed August 5, 2004)

Notes 141

12. Phelps, David, May 13, 2003, "Four former governors beg to differ," *Star Tribune*
13. Lopez, Patricia and Dane Smith, June 29, 2003, "Budget heralds new era in state," *Star Tribune*
14. *Star Tribune*, February 14, 2003, "Aid to cities—Awada both incites, illuminates" editorial
15. deFiebre, Conrad, Revel, May 31, 2003, "Revelry, rivalries echo in chambers," *Star Tribune*
16. Lonetree, Anthony, December 7, 2003, "No outcry over property taxes," *Star Tribune*
17. Howatt, Glenn, June 4, 2003, "State revises cuts to health programs," *Star Tribune*
18. Cummins, H. J., June 5, 2003, "State health cuts hitting home," *Star Tribune*
19. Lopez, Patricia, November 25, 2003, "MinnesotaCare benefit cuts hit diabetics especially hard," *Star Tribune*
20. *Star Tribune*, February 1, 2004, "Sickening cuts—Eventually they will cost more," editorial
21. Lerner, Maura, June 20, 2004, "AIDS drug program faces cuts," *Star Tribune*
22. *Star Tribune*, February 20, 2004, "In-home care—Liens scare elderly away," editorial
23. Minnesota Department of Health Services, Minnesota Health Care Programs, Medical Assistance, http://www.dhs.state.mn.us/main/groups/healthcare/documents/pub/dhs_id_006921.hcsp (accessed August 5, 2004)
24. *Star Tribune*, February 1, 2004, see above
25. Mayron, Amy, September 3, 2003, "Minnesota: Law on legal aid fee voided," *Pioneer Press*
26. Kaszuba, Mike, September 4, 2003, "Fountain fans seek cash flow," *Star Tribune*
27. *Start Tribune*, December 1, 2003, "Minnesota Zoo—Improvements can't wait again" editorial
28. Bentley, Rosalind, February 16, 2004, "Cuts frustrate library patrons," *Star Tribune*
29. Anoka County News, Fall 2003 http://www.anokacounty.us/v1_departments/div-governmental-services/dept-public-information/newsletter/anoka-county-news-2003-fall.pdf (accessed August 5, 2004)
30. Franklin, Robert, November 27, 2003, "Belgrade to pursue DWI case after dropping it because of cost," *Star Tribune*
31. Powell, Joy, March 1, 2004, "Doing more with less," *Star Tribune*

32. Xiong, Chao, June 16, 2004, "Local Habitat for Humanity plans layoffs to cut costs," *Star Tribune*
33. Twin Cities Habitat for Humanity website: http://www.tchabitat.org/habifacts.asp (accessed August 5, 2004)
34. Collins, Terry, June 16, 2004, "Tenants protest cut in rent assistance," *Star Tribune*
35. Medrano Leslie, Lourdes, May 14, 2003, "Mentoring program is finding itself at risk," *Star Tribune*
36. Werner, Larry, July 17, 2003, "Nipped in the bud," *Star Tribune*
37. Grow, Doug, January 29, 2004, "More goodwill is evaporating," *Star Tribune*
38. Franklin, Robert, March 11, 2003, "Catholic Charities cuts 88 jobs as donations decline," *Star Tribune*
39. Greater Minneapolis Council of Churches, January/February 2004 "Chaplaincy cut; short reprieve offered," *Expressions* Vol 13, No. 1, and Highlights from March 23, 2004, meeting of the Hennepin County Board of Commissioners http://www.co.hennepin.mn.us/vgn/portal/internet/hcdetailmaster/0,2300,1273_100496343_103341818,00.html#chaplain (accessed August 8, 2004) and personal communication
40. Hopfensperger, Jean, June 1, 2004, "Faith-based grants flow to Minnesota," *Star Tribune*
41. Hopfensperger, Jean, January 30, 2004, "Child-care cuts sting families, report says," *Star Tribune*
42. *Star Tribune*, September 21, 2003, "Day care conundrum—Legislature made shortsighted cuts" editorial
43. *Star Tribune*, February 8, 2004, "K–12 education—Undermining proven programs" editorial
44. Brandt, Steve, June 28, 2004, "Minneapolis schools face 4th year of cuts," *Star Tribune*
45. Steward, Jamaica, July 6, 2004, "Budget cuts mean class size surplus," *Star Tribune*
46. McAuliffe, Bill, February 29, 2004, "Suburbs, too, closing schools," *Star Tribune*
47. *Star Tribune*, April 20, 2003, "Budget squeeze—The cuts look real in Anoka County" editorial
48. Kumar, Kavita, April 25, 2003, "Private fundraisers boost public schools," *Star Tribune*

49. Lonetree, Anthony, July 17, 2003, "MnSCU students face more tuition increases," *Star Tribune*
50. Coleman, Nick, February 11, 2004, "Education taking big hits in Minneapolis," *Star Tribune*
51. Coleman, Nick, May 14, 2004, "It May Take Prayer to Stop These Folks," *Star Tribune*
52. Smith, Dane, June 17, 2004, "At 95, Anderson offers experience of his years," *Star Tribune*
53. Meyers, Mike, September 29, 2002, "Minnesota is hardest-working state," *Star Tribune*

NOTES ON CHAPTER EIGHT

1. The Taxpayer Protection Pledge was started in 1986 as the first project of Americans for Tax Reform. See http://www.atr.org/nationalpledge/index.html (accessed August 6, 2004)
2. NOW with Bill Moyers, January 10, 2003, "Bill Moyers Interviews Grover Norquist," Public Affairs Television., transcript at http://www.pbs.org/now/transcript/transcript202_full.html (accessed August 6, 2004)
3. from Letter to Share Owners, GE Annual Report, 2000, http://www.ge.com/annual00/letter/page3.html (accessed August 6, 2004)
4. Kamensky, John, April 1997, "The U.S. Reform Experience: The National Performance Review, U.S. Office of Management and Budget, Presentation Notes, Plenary Session, Conference on Civil Service Systems in Comparative Perspectives," Indiana University, Bloomington IN accessible at http://www.indiana.edu/~csrc/kamen1.html (accessed August 6, 2004)
5. Kamensky, John, April 1997, see above
6. Osborne, David, Jan 2000, "For a sneak preview of the American government of the 21st century, look overseas," *Government Executive*, Vol 32, Iss. 1
7. Osborne, David, Jan 2000, see above
8. Osborne, David, Jan 2000, see above
9. Marshall, Joshua Micah, Laura Rozen, and Colin Soloway, December 2003, "The Washington Monthly's Who Who," *The Washington Monthly*
10. Osborne, David, Jan 2000, see above

11. Walters, Jonathan, May 2003, "Civil Service Tsunami—Florida's radical overhaul of its personnel system is making big political waves." *Governing*, Congressional Quarterly, Inc.
12. http://www2.whoseflorida.com/ (accessed August 6, 2004)
13. Franklin, Robert, May 26, 2004, "Times tough for charities that rely on long-term help," *Star Tribune*
14. Salamon, Lester M., May 2002, "Social Engagement," *Foreign Policy*
15. measured as full-time-equivalents as percent of total non-farm employment
16. Rector, Robert, 1995, "How 'Poor' Are America's Poor," in *The state of humanity*, Julian L Simon, ed., Cambridge MA, Blackwell Publishers, Inc.
17. Harney, Kenneth, July 10, 2004, "Load program would assist public servants—Plan to help poorly paid champions," *Star Tribune*

NOTES TO APPENDIX I

1. The source of data on private philanthropy used by *Statistical Abstract of the United States*, 2003, Table No. 581, Private Philanthropy Funds by Source and Allocation: 1990 to 2002 is AAFRC Trust for Philanthropy, researched and written by the Center on Philanthropy at Indiana University, Indianapolis, IN in their publication, *Giving USA*, published annually.
2. *Giving USA 2003*, a publication of the AAFRC Trust for Philanthropy, researched and written by the Center for Philanthropy at Indiana University, Indianapolis, IN
3. *Giving USA 2003*, see above. Descriptions of organization types are based upon those in this text.
4. Hodkinson, Virginia A and Murray S. Weitzman, 1993, *From Belief to Commitment: The Community Service Activities and Finances of Religious Congregations in the United States*, INDEPENDENT SECTOR, Washington D.C.
5. Weiner, Susan J. et al, 2001, *Balancing the Scales: Measuring the Contributions of Nonprofit Organizations and Religious Congregations*, Washington D.C, INDEPENDENT SECTOR
6. Salamon, Lester M., 1999, *America's nonprofit sector: a primer*, 2nd edition, New York, NY, The Foundation Center
7. LaRue, John C., Oct 2002, "Current Research Data on Churches, Where does donated money go?" *Christianity Today*
8. Hoge, Dean R., Charles Zech, Patrick McNamara, and Michael J. Donahue, 1996,

Money Matters: Personal Giving in American Churches, Louisville, KY, Westminster John Knox Press

9. Lindner, Eileen W. ed., 2003, *Yearbook of American and Canadian Churches*, Nashville TN, Abingdon Press, annual. Note correction of 2002 reporting discussed on page 14.
10. Cnaan, Ram, 1999, "Our Hidden Safety Net," *Brookings Review*, Vol 17 i2 p50(1)
11. Chaves, Mark and William Tsitsos, 2001, "Congregations and Social Services: What They Do, How They Do It, and With Whom," Nonprofit Sector Research Fund, Working Paper Series, Washington D.C., The Aspen Institute
12. Reed, Eric, Summer 2000, "Where the Money Goes," *Leadership Journal*, • Vol. XXI, No. 3, Page 88
13. Hoge, Dean R., Charles Zech, Patrick McNamara, and Michael J. Donahue, 1996, see above, page 15, footnote 9
14. Hoge, Dean R., Charles Zech, Patrick McNamara, and Michael J. Donahue, 1996, see above, page 209
15. *Giving USA 2003*, page 133, see above.
16. *Giving USA 2003*, page 137, see above.
17. *Giving USA 2003*, page 151, see above.
18. *Giving USA 2003*, page 156, see above.
19. Based on the average social service expenditures of six, major metropolitan area Federations / United Jewish Appeals
20. *Giving USA 2001*, page 94, see above.
21. *Giving USA 2003*, page 120, see above.
22. *Giving USA 2003*, page 129, see above.
23. *Giving USA 1999*, page 83, see above.
24. The Foundation Center, "Foundations Grants Designated for Special Populations Groups, circa 2000," based on grants of $10,000 or more awarded by a national sample of 1,015 larger U.S. foundations, Foundation Center Statistical Services, http://fdncenter.org/fc_stats/pdf/08_fund_pop/2000/16_00.pdf (accessed August 4, 2004)
25. The Foundation Center, "Distribution of Foundation Grants by Subject Categories, circa 2000," based on grants of $10,000 or more awarded by a national sample of 1,015 larger U.S. foundations, Foundation Center Statistical Services, http://fdncenter.org/fc_stats/pdf/04_fund_sub/2000/10_00.pdf (accessed August 4, 2004)

Index

ACSI. *See* American Customer Satisfaction Index
air quality, 42, 44
American Customer Satisfaction Index, 51
American Lung Association, 44
Americans for Tax Reform. *See* Norquist, Grover
ATR. *See* Americans for Tax Reform
automobile safety, 36

BBBS. *See* Big Brothers Big Sisters
benefits in 2000
    government to those with limited income, 71
    state and local government to those with limited income, 71
Big Brothers Big Sisters, 82
    outcome study, 82
Bush, President George W.
    opposition to tax increase, 106
    signer of no tax increase pledge, 104
    tax cut reasons, 103

Canadian national insurance program administrative costs, 52
CDC. *See* Center for Disease Control
Celtic Tiger. *See* Ireland
Center for Disease Control, 40

charitable contribution estimate
    Education portion to those with limited income, 125
    foundations portion to those with limited income, 125
    Health portion to those with limited income, 125
    Human Service portion to to those with limited income, 124
    Public Society Benefit portion to those with limited income, 124
    Religion, portion to those with limited income, 123
    upper limit estimate of portion to those with limited income, 119, 127
charitable contributions
    categories of, 120
    destination of funds in 2000, 73
    disaster relief public vs. private, 78
    effect of shrinking public budgets, 77
    effect of tragic event, 75
    estimate of upper limit of giving to those with limited income, 119, 127
    from all sources in 2000, 72
    new needs competing with traditional, 76, 114
    percent of church expenditures to those with limited income, 120

private sector limitation, 74, 75, 114
proposed tax changes to promote, 74
Chaves, Mark and William Tsitsos
    Cnaan, Ram studies compared, 84
    houses of worship study, 84
childhood diseases
    eradication, 39
    vaccination programs, 40
civil service
    contractors and, 50
    grant recipients and, 50
    President Carter campaign against, 49
    President Reagan campaign against, 50
    size of federal, 50
Cnaan, Ram
    congregational social services, 120
Cnaan, Ram and S. Boddie
    congregation study, 84
commerce
    freedom restricted, 35
conservative
    beliefs, 3, 4
    plan to dismantle the New Deal, 118
    stress on values, 118
    tradeoff, 118
Consumer Product Safety Commission, 36
consumer protection, 36
    rationale, 107
contractors, government, 50
    criminal or delinquent, 62, 112
    number of, 50
    tax cheating and, 62, 112
contributions to the needy in the year 2000
    estimate, 73

contributions to those with limited income
    estimate of private, 73-74
    public vs. private, 74
Council of State Governments
    survey by, 60
Cronyism
    Coalition Provisional Authority in Iraq, 112
CSG. *See* Council of State Governments

DARPA. *See* Defense Advanced Research Projects Agency
debt of government
    Republican vs Democrat, 106
defense
    role of government, 48
Defense Advanced Research Projects Agency, 34
deviation from GDP trend. *See* business cycle
Dilulio Jr,. Professor John J., 82
disaster relief, 78
disconnected youth, 83
double taxation, 106

economic expansion
    peace-time, 15
economic expansion in the 1990s
    employee shortage, 104
economic growth
    tax burden and, 25
Edison Schools, 66
    Philadelphia Public Schools, 66
education
    See also public sector investment
    for profit enterprises, 65
    high school graduates in 1900, 32

high school graduation changes during the 20th century, 33
  in 1900, 29
  post-secondary development, 33
  productivity and, 34
  Sputnik and, 33
efficiency
  private sector, 57
employee shortage in 1990s, 11
Erie Canal, 31

faith
  effect of. *See* religious commitment
faith-based initiatives, 79-85, 114
  competition with for profit organizations, 115
  sustained attention and, 81
Food and Drug Act, 36
Framingham Heart Study, 40
freedom
  commerce restrictions, 35
  contribution of public investment, 107
  contribution of public investment to, 30-35
freedom in 2000, 30

G.I. Bill of Rights, 33
GDP
  and tax burden. *See* tax burden
  defined, 11
GE. *See* Welch, Jack
  improvement inititatives, 56
General Electric Corporation. *See* GE
government reform
  Al Gore, 110
  Clinton initiatives, 110
  David Osborne, 110
  Florida, 113
  Great Britain, 110
  lack of employee protection in Florida, 113
  National Performance Review principles, 110
  New Zealand, 110
  protecting employees, 111
  smaller and stronger effect, 111
government size
true size in 2002, 50
Gross domestic product
  defined. *See* GDP

Head Start, 41
health care
  national systems and standard of living, 23
  U.S. as percent of GDP, 23
Hong Kong, 21
houses of worship
  collaboration with other organizations, 84
  help for needy, types of, 84

IMF, 22
income tax in 1900, 30
Index of Economic Freedom
  countries with high tax burdens and, 105
  defined, 18
  Denmark and, 18
  free economies, 23
  Heritage Foundation and, 18
  Hong Kong and, 18
  Singapore and, 18
  Sweden and, 18
  Wall Street Journal and, 18

information technology
    defined, 58
International Monetary Fund. *See* IMF
Interstate Highway Act of 1956, 31
interstate highway system
    and increased choices, 31
    economic effects, 31
Ireland, 26
IT. *See* information technology

law enforcement
    role of government, 48
Lean Manufacturing, 56
life expectancy
    current, 39
    health improvement and, 41
    in 1900, 30
    in 2000, 30
life in the year 1900, 29
Luxembourg, 22

Marshall Plan, 46
Medicare
    administrative costs, 52
    compared to private insurers, 52
    customer satisfaction, 52
mentoring
    Big Brothers Big Sisters effect of, 82
    difficulty finding volunteers, 82, 83
    effect, 81
    Prison Fellowship Ministries and, 81
Minnesota
    chaplaincy budget pressures, 96
    child care subsidies reduced, 97
    education budget cuts, 97
    election of 2002, 89
    faith-based grants received, 97
    frail elderly assistance changes 2003–2004, 92
    health care changes 2003-2004, 91
    hunting season for mourning doves adopted in 2004, 100
    legislative gridlock in 2004, 99
    liberal history, 87
    libraries, effect of budget cuts, 94
    non-budget legislation 2003, 91
    non-profits, effect of recession and budget cuts, 94
    on top ten lists, 88
    public defender, increased charges for 93
    Republicans, 87, 90
    Republicans, right wing, 91, 100
    third parties, 89
Minnesota governors
    past criticize present, 90, 100
Minnesota state auditor
    definition of essential services, 91

National Defense Education Act of 1958, 33
National Institutes of Health, 40
National Park Service, 47
national parks, 47, 108
National Review, 1
National Science Foundation, 34
NIH. *See* National Institutes of Health
Norquist, Grover
    "leave us alone" coalition, 4
    goal of reducing government, 107
    Taxpayer Protection Pledge, 103
NPS. *See* National Park Service
NSF. *See* National Science Foundation

OECD, 18, 22
Organization for Economic Cooperation and Development
    defined. *See* OECD

organizational culture, 57
organizational efficiency
    in public and private organizations, 108
    private sector, 57
outsourcing
    business processes, 58
    by foreign governments, 59
    conservative hopes for, 57, 111
    cost savings, 59-60, 111
    defined, 57
    federal government recent, 60
    government processes, 58
    military, 61
    reasons to, 58
    state government use, 60

patent growth in the twentieth century. *See* tax burden
Pendleton Act, 49
pesticides
    regulation, 36
PFM. *See* Prison Fellowship Ministries
philanthropy. *See* charitable contributions
place to live. See quality of life
POGO. *See* Project on Government Oversight
pollution. also *See* regulation
    air, 42, 44
poverty
    affordable housing lack, 117
    needs filled inexpensively, 117
    needs that are costly, 117
    redefinition, 116
    redefinition in Minnesota, 93
PPP. *See* purchasing power parity
President Hoover
    administrator of grants and loans, 70
    opposition to welfare, 70

President Reagan, 1
    quoted, 3
    use of debt as restraint, 106
Prison Fellowship Ministries, 80
    Texas prison project, 81
prison privatization, 63-65
private sector efficiency, 52
Project on Government Oversight, 62
public safety
    role of government, 48
public sector investment
    education, 32
    education in the Kennedy-Johnson years, 33
    G.I. Bill of Rights, 33
    health improvement and longevity, 107
    increased worker productivity, 34
    Internet, 35
    National Defense Education Act of 1958, 33
    post-Sputnik, 33
    research, basic, 34, 107
    research, medical, 40
    roads, highways, bridges, 31
purchasing power parity
    defined, 22

quality of life,
    factors affecting, 42-44
quality principles, 53, 109

regulation
    automobile safety, 36
    biblical, 36
    consumer products. *See* Consumer Product Safety Commission
    food and drug, 36, 37
    pesticides, 36

pollution, 42, 108
stocks and bonds, 37
religious commitment
    alcohol abuse, effect on, 83
    delinquency, effect on, 83
    drug use, effect on, 83
    inner-city youths effect on, 83
research
    government role in, 34, 40
    medical, 40
return on investment
    early childhood education, 41, 108
    vaccinations, 41
right wing. *See* conservative

school privatization, 65-68
schools
    for profit. *See* Edison Schools
SEC. *See* Securities and Exchange Commission
Securities and Exchange Commission, 37
    underfunding, 38
Six Sigma, 55
    savings realized by GE, 56
Social Security, 44
    public acceptance of, 44
    Trustees prediction, 44
Social Security Administration, 51
    administrative costs, 51
    customer satisfaction, 51
space program, 45, 108
SSA. *See* Social Security Administration
standard of living
    economic growth and, 26
    nations with low, 24
    nations with mid-range, 24
    tax burden and, 15
    top ten for the year 2000, 23

tax burden
    business cycle and, 15
    defined by OECD, 18
    defined by Tax Foundation, 7
    economic growth and, 19, 25, 105
    federal portion, 9
    GDP, real and, 11
    growth of patents and, 11
    in 2000, 30
    longest peacetime expansion and, 15, 104
    nationalized health care and, 23
    nations with high standard of living, 23
    nations with highest, 18
    nations with low standard of living, 24
    nations with mid-range standard of living, 24
    real GDP and, 11, 104
    standard of living and, 15
    state and local portion, 11
    twentieth century, 7
Tax Foundation, 7
Tax Freedom Day, 7
Tax Reform Act of 1986, 105
Taxpayers League of Minnesota, 89
    Taxpayer Protection Pledge, 89
    transportation plan for the poor, 90
Teen Challenge, 80
    length of stay study outcomes, 80
traffic congestion, 32
transportation system
    failure to maintain, 32

vaccination program, 40
volunteers
    difficulty finding, 115
    European, 115

Wackenhut Corporation, 63
war memorials. *See* national parks
Welch, Jack
    attitude to improvement, 56
    introduces Six Sigma, 56
welfare
    government funds spent in 2000, 71
    history of government involvement, 69
    retreat of the Right from, 116
work week
    after 1938, 30
    in 1900, 29

Xerox Corporation, 53-55
    competition from Japan 1982, 53
    GE Capital assists, 54
    Malcolm Baldridge award, 54